The Gardens of
MADEIRA

The Gardens of
MADEIRA

GERALD LUCKHURST

F

FRANCES LINCOLN LIMITED
PUBLISHERS

For my wife, Paula

Frances Lincoln Limited
4 Torriano Mews
Torriano Avenue
London NW5 2RZ
www.franceslincoln.com

A catalogue record for this book is available from the
British Library.

978-0-7112-3032-3

Printed and bound in China

1 2 3 4 5 6 7 8 9

Commissioned and edited by Jane Crawley

HALF-TITLE Jardim da Senhora at the Blandy Gardens.
TITLE PAGE Dragon Tree Sanctuary.
RIGHT Rose garden at Quinta do Arco.

Contents

Preface

Darwin was the first to notice how island floras, isolated from related populations, developed their own characteristics and became unique. The island gardens of Madeira are unique, but for quite the opposite reason. For hundreds of years they were at the crossroads of the world; a traveller's cosmopolitan style developed, populated by ideas and plants from all across the globe. As a half-way-house between the tropics and the old continent, Madeira received plants from far-flung empires and accommodated ideas from both north and south.

A sort of hothouse *gardenesque* produced gardens and parks overflowing with palms, orchids and bamboos. Gingerbread houses with wide verandas looked out over spacious lawns, patterned with island beds of exotic foliage and brightly coloured flowers. Fruits from the four corners of the earth lent a taste of Eden, and giant tortoises, tree ferns, and cycads made a primeval impression.

The colonial style persisted well into the twentieth century, along with a genteel tourism of retired military personnel and East Indiamen. But Madeira was no longer on international trade routes. In isolation from new ideas and development, ideas long abandoned as old-fashioned in European gardens crystallised into a Madeira garden style. The influx of new plants, however, continued; Madeira is a land of emigration, with large populations in South Africa, Brazil and even Hawaii. As emigrants returned home they brought with them botanic souvenirs. The Madeira tourist, nature-loving and generally grey-haired, has now reversed the flow of botanic souvenirs, going home laden with orchids, strelitzias and exotic fruits.

The development of modern tourism has brought new impetus to the island's gardens. Madeira now promotes itself as the garden of the Atlantic, new hotels compete amongst themselves for the showiest display, and an annual flower festival has become the most popular event of the tourist calendar. As new roads and tunnels have improved

internal communications, so other gardens have been built to attract visitors to remoter parts of the island.

The climate of Madeira makes gardening easy. In comparison with mainland Portugal, where plants struggle to survive summer drought, growth is abundant, and everyone has a green thumb. This has instilled a native love of plants that is quite uncharacteristic of southern latitudes. The gardens of Madeira are not confined to grand houses and fine hotels – each patio and stairway is crammed with pots, the vineyards and country roadsides are brimming with flowers. The streets and squares of the towns are filled with magnificent trees (jacarandas, flame trees and rosewoods) and even the waterways are covered by trellises of bougainvillea.

I have been making gardens in Madeira since 1991, nearly twenty years. It has been an exercise in choice, growing plants from all over the world and learning from devoted growers who live on the island. Visiting these Madeira gardens, researching their history and photographing them has been a happy task and one that I have enjoyed sharing with many friends and colleagues. I hope that this book will allow me to convey my enthusiasm further afield. My thanks are due to each of the garden owners and managers and in particular I should like to acknowledge the encouragement and support of Dionisio Pestana, without whom this book could never have been written.

The book begins with an introduction to the discovery and development of the island and its earliest gardens. It covers the role of Portuguese aristocrats and British wine merchants in creating the country estates known as quintas and uses the extensive travel literature of early tourists to illustrate their features. The climate and landscape of Madeira and the unique flora are briefly considered as essential background for visitors to the gardens which are then individually described.

Introduction

The legendary Gardens of the Hesperides lay in islands of the western ocean, far beyond the setting sun, where fearsome dragons guarded golden apples. The first navigators exploring the Atlantic Ocean were wary of what they might encounter. But there were no dragons on Madeira, only trees that oozed their vinous blood, and rather than gardens, the explorers found eerily quiet woodlands. The discovery of Madeira, and the cultivation of its landscape, is wrapped in myth, indeed legend, and even today the island still conveys the image of a paradise garden.

As early as 1351 a Genoese map, the *Laurentian portolano*, bore an indication of the *Isola della Lolegname* – the island of wood. When translated into Portuguese this became simply, *Madeira* (timber). Established by Zarco, who rediscovered the island in 1419, the Portuguese expedition flourished, and the first children born on the island were twins. Symbolically they were baptised Adam and Eve.

But this was no Eden, for the first settlers had to look to their survival and to their sustenance. They burnt the primeval forest to clear land for crops. The chronicles state that fires raged for seven years. Once cleared the initial yields from virgin soils were high. One grain sown in the field yielded ten or twenty more on harvest. Soon vines were planted too, providing for the Christian ritual, as well as helping to keep up spirits.

The first economy was based upon the export of timber, dragon's blood (from the resin of those strange trees that grew on the sea cliffs), and precious wheat exported to the motherland. But after a while the colony was able to look to more profitable cultures, and there began the cycle of cash crops that was to characterise the agriculture of the island to the present day. The first of these crops was sugar cane, introduced from Sicily as early as 1452 by Prince Henry the Navigator. In the sixteenth and seventeenth centuries

RIGHT The Penha d'Aguia (Eagle Rock) with the Ponta de São Lourenço in the distance seen from the Quinta do Furão. The northern coast of Madeira is full of such magnificent landscapes.

ABOVE Bananas flourish among flowering shrubs: *Tibouchina grandifolia* and *Nerium oleander* in the garden of the Pestana Village hotel.

RIGHT A forest of dragon trees once covered the southern coastline. At the Dragon Tree Sanctuary these giants may still be seen in association with natural vegetation.

Madeira grew rich from this 'white gold'. This led to the establishment of the first noble houses and a flourishing of the arts, and also, as life became easier, to the making of gardens. Naturally these gardens were dominated by food production, and the earliest references to garden plants are generally to fruits, rather than to flowers. The banana was introduced from Asia in the sixteenth century.

A description of the Island of Madeira in a letter to a friend, printed in 1748, but based on a number of earlier sources including the *Descritione dell Isola d'illa Madera scrita nella lingua latina* by Conte Giulio Landi (Piacenza, 1574), gives a delightful description of these early gardens and of the abundance of exotic fruits then grown. 'The island abounds with fruits of various kinds, and most delicious to the taste; bananas, opuntias, yams, guavas, figs, quinces, apples, bays, oranges, limes, dates and citrons, chestnuts, walnuts, and kitchen fruits in great quantities....' The reference to citron is particularly interesting, since this was the basis of an important industry. Locally produced sugar was used to candy these and other fruits for export.

The fruit of the banana tree in 'shape and size resembles our cucumber. It is of an oily saponaceous, and luscious nature, which renders the taste at first disagreeable;

BELOW A clutch of topiary
hens nestle around a shallow
stone pool at the Quinta
do Palheiro Ferreiro
(Blandy Gardens).

but when become more familiar, it proves more delicious.' Pineapples were grown, but only in 'particular gardens', and the true cinnamon tree, brought from the East Indies to Brazil and thence to Madeira, was now growing in the garden of the *Providore*. The letter ends with a description of a tree that grew all over the island, 'from which the dragon's blood is procured'. It was considered a sovereign remedy for bruises.

Madeira exported its sugar know-how and planters to Brazil and soon, with more favourable conditions and a slave economy, sugar was produced there at far more competitive rates. The Madeira islanders turned their attention to wine production. By 1687 Sir Hans Sloane reported that 'the greatest part of the island is at present planted by vines'. A small community of foreign wine traders began to establish themselves. 'The Merchant is thriving and Rich, whilst the Grape-gatherer imploy'd by him, is but Poor,' reported John Ovington in 1689. Later, in the eighteenth century, the wars between France and England and the consequent

blockade of French ports gave a much needed boost to the popularity of Madeira wine. In particular, America became a favoured market.

The Napoleonic Wars brought other changes to Madeira leading to the occupation of the islands by the British, first for a short period in 1801–2 and then from 1807 until 1814. British interests, both commercial and social, shaped much of the island's destiny.

In 1804, the most important of Madeira's historic gardens was founded, the Quinta do Palheiro Ferreiro (now known as Blandy Gardens). Its owner, João Esmeraldo, a local nobleman, was culturally influenced by the French, but politically allied to the British. These tendencies were to dominate Madeira, indeed the whole of Portugal, throughout the nineteenth century.

Perhaps the most significant garden maker of the early nineteenth century was Henry Veitch, the British consul. Too colourful a character to succeed as a diplomat (he was a Freemason, sacked for fraternising with Napoleon on his way to exile

LEFT A torrent of blue
and white hydrangeas and
agapanthus flows down
the hillsides of the Public
Garden at Monte.

in Saint Helena), he used his position and fortune gained from the wine trade to build a series of beautiful classical houses and their accompanying gardens. (He was, in fact, an amateur architect – see English Church, pp.48–9) He is buried under a monument that he designed at the Quinta do Jardim da Serra.

Madeira – as a favoured port of call for all those setting south – was visited and described by many famous navigators and explorers: Lord Anson in 1740, Captain Cook in 1768 and 1772, right up to Robert Scott and Amundsen of Antarctica, both of whom came in 1910. Often these voyagers were accompanied by naturalists, Joseph Banks and Daniel Solander came with Cook and Charles Darwin on the *Beagle* in 1832. Darwin in fact never landed, and his knowledge of the island was based on correspondence with the island's naturalists, of whom there were many, such as the botanist the Rev. R. T. Lowe and the entomologist Thomas Vernon Wollaston. Among the first plant collectors were Francis Masson, sent out by Kew in 1776 and again in 1783, and Robert Brown en route to Australia in 1809. Friedrich Welwitsch, an Austrian botanist who made important plant collections in Africa, passed through in 1853 on his way to Angola.

The favourable climate of the island began to be promoted as a salvation for those afflicted by respiratory complaints. That this was but a temporary relief is attested by the Old Burial Ground, whose garden is described in a later chapter (see pp.48–9): 'The English place of interment – a small gloomy spot, with straight walks and rows of cypress... I felt, as I looked at the crowded tombs, that my own might, not long hence, be amongst them' (from the *Journal* of Emily Shore). These consumptive travellers are however of great interest to the history of Madeira's gardens for they were, in general, highly educated and literate travellers, many of whom left accounts in letters and journals of what they saw.

Emily Shore, a little known poet, came to the island in 1838, when she was but nineteen and died in the following year. She excitedly described her first glimpse of a Madeira garden from the windows of her lodging house:

…with delighted astonishment we looked down on a garden crowded with the richest green foliage….I do not think that any garden was ever so charming in my eyes…a carpet of vines covering the trellis-work shaded the walks. Orange trees, five and twenty feet in height, loaded with golden fruit, light bamboos, bananas with their broad-fringed leaves, thick-leafy coffee trees, forming an impenetrable and evergreen shade, camellias of enormous size, china roses still in bloom – all combined in a completely foreign picture from anything I ever saw.

Such descriptions were repeated a hundred times, almost word for word. Breakfast tables laden with exotic fruit, delicious coffee (Veitch noted that the backyards of Funchal produced over 2,000 pounds of roasted beans a year), melodious canaries in the trees; all were eager consolation to these melancholy souls. Freshly revitalised, some would take to their pony and visit the hills above Funchal and explore the majestic scenery of the Corral, a cauldron-like valley high in the mountains that was the obligatory destination for all romantic tourists.

It is from these descriptions that a generalised picture of the gardens and streets of Funchal may be obtained. The gardens were surrounded by high walls, painted yellow ochre with rust red bands along the base and as trim around doors and windows. The narrow streets between these walls were far from dull since the contents of the exuberant gardens escaped over the confining walls: hedges of fuchsia, heliotrope and roses mixed with geraniums, gardenias and jasmine

ABOVE Funchal harbour seen from a garden *mirante* in 1852. From *Views in Madeira* by the Norwegian artist Johan Fredrik Eckersberg.

BELOW *Strelitzia reginae* drawn by Augusta Robley for *A selection of Madeira flowers*, 1845, which she dedicated to her mother, Jane Wallas Penfold.

tumbled out. Often vine-clad pergolas would bridge over the roads. The taller trees such as bitter oranges and loquats would bend into the street under the weight of their abundant fruit.

Leaving Funchal, travellers would pass through country roads barely paved with shards of black basalt. (Or worse, none at all; opinion as to the state of the roads is unanimous. It is said that there were no wheeled vehicles on Madeira for this reason.) The estates around the town were known as *Quintas* (pronounced as often spelt by early English writers: *Kintas*). These are country houses, originally farms, equivalent to modest Italian villas. Each property would have a small area around the house known as the *jardim* (garden) surrounded by far more extensive areas of vineyards and vegetable gardens known as the *fazenda*. By force of necessity this land would be terraced and great retaining walls are a feature of the Madeira landscape. The garden would contain pretty flower beds edged with box or myrtle and the walls surrounding the enclosures would be decorated with niches and benches, sometimes with painted tiles (*azulejos*) but these were an imported luxury, more often broken crockery and volcanic tuff was used to create grottos. The paving in these enclosed areas was characteristically laid out in patterns of tiny black pebbles carried up from riverbeds or the beach.

A unique and ubiquitous feature of these gardens was the *Casinha de Prazer*.

ABOVE A modern-day
mirante in the Quinta
Pestana (a garden designed
by Gerald Luckhurst).

The name means 'pleasure house' and is derived from the French *maison de plaisance*, a term used for garden buildings and banqueting houses since the seventeenth century. Characteristically these little summer houses were located at the corner of the property, perched atop high walls, and always overlooking the street and views beyond. Before the summer houses became fashionable *mirantes* or *miradouros* (viewing platforms often covered by vine pergolas) were used in the same way.

The British tourists describe how the commotion caused by the clatter of their ponies' hooves invariably led to dark-eyed beauties peering at them through the slats of these summer-house windows. Young women of Portuguese society led extremely sheltered lives, leaving their homes only to attend Mass. The view of the street offered release from their flowery prisons.

Many of these quintas were rented by their aristocratic Portuguese owners to British shippers and seasonal visitors. In 1845 Jeanne Wallas Penfold published an album of botanical watercolours depicting fruits and flowers from her garden at the Quinta da Achada. The book tells how some of the plants were introduced to the island's gardens by her friends. Geraniums and succulents were brought from South Africa, fuchsias and heliotropes from South America, agaves and salvias from Mexico and later from Australia arrived tree ferns, mimosas and eucalypts.

As early as 1757 Richard Carlos Smith founded a 'garden of acclimatisation'

ABOVE Clouds hanging on the mountain top at Pico do Areeiro.

RIGHT The *Capacete* or helmet as seen on the mountains above the Quinta de Santo António.

as nursery to receive and re-export exotic plants, principally from South Africa. In 1797 Domingos Vandelli (keeper of the Lisbon botanic garden) and João Carlos Oliveira set up a botanic garden that was maintained until 1828.

The climate of Madeira may be classified as somewhere between subtropical and temperate. The island's relatively small land mass does not heat up excessively and temperatures are tempered by the sea both in summer and winter. This has a marked effect upon seasonality, differences between extremes are slight. Storms that affect the southern coasts in winter are caused by a shift in trade winds.

In mountainous areas there are winter snowfalls, but average winter temperatures in Funchal are only a few degrees below summer figures. A dirty dry wind that occasionally blows from the east in summer is known as '*l'Este*'. This originates from the Sahara and, alarmingly for gardeners, it can also bring swarms of locusts. In fact these cause little damage as most drop dead from exhaustion. The real harm is from the periods of great heat and very low humidity that accompany this wind.

The north-east trade winds that blow in spring and summer carry warm and humid air from the sea. Forced to rise by mountain ranges, water in the air condenses to form clouds and fog. In the north of the island clouds are frequent from midday onwards. The clouds hang at about 1,300m, kept in place by cooler air above. These clouds are known as the '*Capacete*' (helmet), and can often be seen from Funchal, though rarely descending to the south coast.

The mountain range that divides the island protects the southern half from heavy winds and clouds are much less frequent. Consequently there are about double the hours of sunshine and a much drier climate. Funchal has an average annual rainfall

RIGHT The dramatic mountain landscape of the Pico do Areeiro illustrates many features of volcanic geology. It is a favoured destination for walkers.

of 500–600 mm. In the highlands from 2,300–3,200mm may be expected, as much as a tropical rain forest.

The red soils derive from erosion of the volcanic rocks. Chemical changes wrought upon ash, lava, cinders, tuff and basalt, together with biological agents result in the formation of a red clay-like soil. The bright colour is derived from the iron oxides that it contains. It is a myth that these soils are extremely fertile. High temperatures generate a great deal of microbial activity in the soil that consumes nutrients and organic matter is very low. Madeira gardens must be well nourished and watered if they are to thrive.

Although it is only a small island, the volcanic landscape of Madeira is grandiose. The height of the mountains is often not apparent from Funchal since they are hidden amidst the clouds. Indeed often the view from Madeira's highest peak (*Areeiro*, nearly 2,000m) is like that from an aeroplane – above the clouds. Deep ravines bisect the mountains and here the landscape is truly spectacular. The mountain forests are traversed by a network of *levadas* (irrigation channels) that bring water from the north to the south, allowing easy walking access to the remotest locations. High plateaus above the treeline are covered by misty heaths, seemingly just like Scotland.

The island flora can be divided in different layers, according to altitude. The area of Funchal, and all along the south coast was originally covered by littoral vegetation adapted to hot dry conditions. Typical representatives would be the dragon tree (*Dracaena draco*) and various types of grey-leaved sub-shrubs such as *Helichrysum* and *Euphorbia piscatoria*. There is also a lavender (*Lavandula pinnata*).

It is high in the mountains, amongst the clouds, that the *Laurisilva* forest is to be found. Dense, dark and dank, it is home to many of Madeira's unique species. The trees are mostly evergreens with simple leaves, 'laurels' in common parlance. Here there are also some spectacular herbaceous flowering plants: *Echium candicans, Geranium maderense, Sonchus fruticosus*. Many ferns grow here too. Above the *Laurisilva* there is heath-like vegetation on mountain peaks and plateaus. This is home to tree heathers (*Erica*) and blueberries (*Vaccinium*).

All the gardens described are in or around Funchal, with the exception of the rose garden at Quinta do Arco, which is on the north coast at São Jorge. A drive to this wild and beautiful landscape is not to be missed. Also a few not strictly gardens have been included so as to introduce the wild flora and landscape of Madeira, certainly of interest to garden lovers.

1. Blandy Gardens

Quinta do Palheiro Ferreiro

The Quinta do Palheiro Ferreiro has a history stretching over 200 years. Like many fine gardens it is a palimpsest of garden making by several generations of different families each making its own contribution.

The property was founded in 1791 by João José Xavier do Carvalhal Esmeraldo Vasconcelos de Atouguia Bettencourt Sá Machado (1778–1837). Such a portfolio of names was common amongst Portuguese aristocrats and is an indication of the agglomeration of inheritance that made this young man the wealthiest landowner of his day. He owned about a third of the island of Madeira. The estate, quaintly named after a blacksmith's hut (a *palheiro* is a thatched shelter), had its origins as a hunting lodge. The house was built in 1804 and extended in the 1820s.

Despite his ancient lineage, Carvalhal was a modern thinker. His support for liberal ideals meant that he was forced to flee the island in 1828 during the Portuguese civil war. He sailed from Madeira on the frigate *Alligator*, sent out by Wellington to protect British interests during the occupation of the island by troops of the absolutist faction. Only in 1834, on the establishment of a constitutional government, was he able to return. He had supported the winning side and for this was made a count. *Carvalhal* means oak: the family title comes from another property at Lombarda.

Fittingly Carvalhal planted many oaks in his new park, but also fir trees which were then fashionable. Tradition has it that the garden was laid out by a French landscape gardener. Two hundred men were employed on the estate. The park was made with broad avenues of plane trees and chestnuts, intersecting walks, fish ponds, flower gardens and on the highest point, the Balancal, an elegant tower was built. This folly, today in ruins, still shows traces of the original neoclassical decoration of fresco columns and plaster garlands. A small chapel, dedicated to St John the Baptist, has survived intact from this time.

The garden became an obligatory destination for all visitors to the island, some of whom described it in letters home. John Driver a resident physician saw the garden in 1834 during the exile of João Carvalhal:

> The park, if we may so term it, is more in the English style than we expected to find it; but when we came to the orange, lemon, pomegranate, and shaddock groves, which were in fine foliage, and planted in the best order, we, at once,

LEFT Cottage garden flowers mingle with rare exotics in the Jardim da Senhora at the Quinta do Palheiro Ferreiro.

ABOVE *Ixia paniculata* is a beautiful bulb from South Africa. Christina Blandy finds it rather troublesome and gardeners have to weed it out.

BELOW *Calceolaria integrifolia* 'Kentish Hero' and *Iresine lindenii* both grow as perennials in the borders of the Jardim da Senhora.

appreciated the effects of this southern clime. The flower gardens, though not abounding in that variety that one might expect, are well arranged; but begin to show more of the 'fallen state' of things than other parts of the house. The flowers that most attracted us were the camellias, which bloomed, in the greatest profusion, in white, crimson, crimson and white, and other colours, on trees upwards of twenty feet in height. Various species of the cactus tribe, and of considerable growth, displayed their beautiful and singular flowers.

An anecdote quoted by other authors tells how the land steward was once instructed to count the camellias. He reached 9,000 and exhaustedly proposed to his master that they should agree on a total of 10,000. Other plants were said to have been introduced following the return of the Portuguese court from Brazil in 1821.

For a man of such wealth the house that Carvalhal had built was modest, yet this it seems was characteristic of his personality: 'built in good style, and is in keeping with the place'. He died a bachelor in 1837. His nephew and heir was quite a different character; gardening is unlikely to have been high on his priorities.

TOP RIGHT The triploid
form of *Kniphofia thompsonii*
brought to the gardens many
years ago by the author.

BOTTOM RIGHT *Felicia
fruticosa* is a little shrubby
daisy that grows in the
sunken garden.

By 1840, just three years after the first count's death, the garden had a desolate air. Robert Burts, a literary U.S. naval officer thought it 'a fit location for Thompson's "Castle of Indolence".'

It was, I ween, a lovely spot of ground;
And there a season atween June and May
Half prankt with spring, with summer half imbrown'd,
A listless climate made, where, sooth to say,
Was nought around but images of rest:
Sleep-soothing groves, and quiet lawns between:
And flowery beds that slumberous influence kest,
From poppies breath'd; and beds of pleasant green.

By 1885 the Carvalhal fortune was all gone. Palheiro was put up for public auction. The buyer was John Burden Blandy (1841–1912). The Blandys had arrived in Madeira at the beginning of the nineteenth century. John Blandy (1783–1855), quartermaster to General Beresford's British force that had occupied Madeira for the second time during the Napoleonic Wars, had seen an opportunity for business and had settled permanently on the island in 1810 with his new wife Jane Burden. For the greater part of the nineteenth century the Blandy fortunes in Madeira had gone in the opposite direction from those of the profligate second count. In particular the Blandys had foreseen the disastrous consequences of the oidium epidemic by buying up the dwindling wine stocks of the island.

Thus firmly established, John Burden Blandy could afford to take a risk. The rest of the family was appalled at what was seen as the purchase of a vainglorious white elephant. The huge estate had been long abandoned and in particular the count's house was in ruinous condition. Lost in the forest of trees planted by the first Carvalhal, it did not even enjoy the views that had been the first attraction for the foundation of the estate.

Blandy, business-minded as always, renovated the pastures, and built new dams, sawmills and outbuildings. He established the farming and forestry activities of the estate producing wheat and fresh vegetables, in addition to a dairy herd. He tried briefly to establish an hotel in the house of the counts – the Casa Velha – but this venture was abandoned when he decided to transform the *palheiro* into a summer residence for his family.

ABOVE Dramatic contrast in form between the succulent *Agave attenuata* and the tall spires of Italian cypress.

RIGHT The new house, designed by Micklethwaite and Somers Clarke, stands at a distance from the gardens surrounded by lawns.

In 1889 JBB (as he was known) decided to build the new house on higher ground, where views of Funchal were more expansive. This was on the site of the Casa da Francesa (a cottage built for the second count's French mistress). The architects were George Somers Clarke, junior (1841–1926) and John Thomas Micklethwaite (1843–1906), who later worked in Madeira as architects of the Reid's New Hotel (opened in 1891). They designed a large Arts and Crafts style cottage, quite a departure for these disciples of George Gilbert Scott who were well-known ecclesiologists. They were in partnership from 1876 to 1892. The Blandy flair for mercantile trade certainly influenced the appearance of the house through manufactured goods imported for its fabric — everything from the chimney-pots to the doormat was brought from England. Local influence is seen through the use of dressed basalt stonework.

The garden laid out around the house was formed of geometric terraces and walks, rather in the line of Reginald Blomfield's *Formal Garden in England*. Blomfield and Micklethwaite collaborated as authors of essays on architecture published in 1892. In this way the architects followed the rectilinear plan of the original garden of the counts. One departure was the development of the Ribeiro do Inferno, a tree fern gulley planted during the early years of the twentieth century. In his book *Leaves from a Madeira garden* (1909), Charles Thomas-Stanford makes an interesting

remark regarding the 'ancient contest between the *formalist* and the *naturalist*'.
Madeira gardens are of necessity formal, 'naturalization' is quite out of place where
the soil has to be held in terraces. The natural treatment of rocky cliffs or ravines on
the boundary of gardens may however, in his judgement, be 'eminently successful'.
In fact the Palheiro garden has, for a mountain garden, an unusual amount of
relatively flat land. The formal treatment probably originated from terraces built
for agriculture that were adapted to gardens.

In 1901 the garden was the setting for a party to entertain King Carlos and
Queen Amelia of Portugal during an official visit to Madeira. Dom Carlos, a rather
overweight sportsman, and smoking a cigar, was diplomatically allowed to win both
tennis matches after lunch in three straight sets.

Four years after that tennis match Mildred Edmonds was born in South Africa.
After her marriage to Graham Blandy she went on to make Palheiro one of the most
celebrated botanical collections in the world.

Mildred Blandy describes her garden in an article she wrote for the September
1955 Royal Horticultural Society Journal. Some of the plants, such as thirty-three
feet (10 metre) high trees of *Camellia sasanqua*, must have been planted before the
Blandy era, and have since disappeared. She notes the count's fine large specimens
of tulip trees, sequoias, ginkgos and cedars that are still with us. But the principal

LEFT A shocking topiary
whatnot made of clipped
Muehlenbeckia complexa with
regal pelargoniums below.

interest of this article is the insight gained concerning the plants that were introduced during her tenure. As a South African it is natural that plants of the Veldt and Cape should have found favour. Short-lived silver trees, *Leucadendron argenteum*, were a feature of her garden. Gleefully she noted that, although South African gardeners considered them impossible to grow outside their native Cape, she had just raised over a hundred new trees from seed collected in the garden.

The sunken garden was an especially favourite area. Terraced banks about eight feet (2.4 metres) in depth were planted with many gaily hued small plants. 'Rock lovers', she called them. All were South African natives: *Nerium appendiculata*, babianas, ixias and sparaxis ('of every colour'), *Tritonia crocata*, *Haemanthus katherinae*, *Aristea capitata*, *Dierama pulcherrima*, *Gladiolus tristis*, *Ursinia anthemoides* and *Arctotis*. And that was just the beginning of the list. Happily many of these little treasures were so at home that they have survived these fifty years.

Just exactly as she describes them are the wild yellow lupins that grow between many varieties of azalea along the stream bank. As are the edging of freesias and scarlet tritonias lining the stream. This is one of the most photographed features of today's garden. The shallow stone pool of the Jardim da Senhora (The Lady's Garden), with the miniature yellow waterlily, has also survived. The pool was surrounded by a knot garden, intensively worked in golden box. This is long gone. Labour was cheap and plentiful in those days.

Mildred Blandy praises the work done by her local gardeners, particularly their skill in topiary work. Her head gardener José was, however, prone to superstition. Planting was always carried out in accordance with the phases of the moon (this is still a widely held creed) and one plant, *Diosma ericoides* was considered a lucky charm to be included in all new flower beds. Decidedly unlucky was her much adored Italian cypress (seed had been brought from the Villa Adriana). According to José these should be consigned to the cemetery. Perhaps this is why few outlived their progenitor.

A walk into the estate today begins at the pretty gatekeeper's lodge; the sensation of translocation to an English park is immediate. The impression is Reptonesque, with delicate iron fences lining the cobbled driveway beneath ancient planes; the dairy cattle that used to browse in their shade have gone, but the atmosphere of these meadows remains bucolic. The floral abundance of these fields is hallucinogenic — each in their season, multitudes of arum lilies, agapanthus or amaryllis joyously transport the mind.

TOP *Calycanthus floridus*, the Carolina allspice.

ABOVE 'Mathotiana', one of the many camellias to be found throughout the gardens.

BELOW A flourish of wrought iron from JBB's gates to the new house.

It is a long walk, and with these ethereal thoughts one can quite forget the outside world. Secrets open at a leisured pace. Glimpses of camellias in the hedgerow and a view of chimney tops announce the arrival of the garden. This is one of the delights of Palheiro, imperceptibly the farmland merges into garden, which in turn peters out to the modern golf course.

On arrival, announced by discordant yellow taxis herded at the gate, views open in three directions. The order of the estate becomes apparent. To the right, the home grounds surrounding the house are barred by wrought-iron gates bearing the monograph of John Blandy. Wide lawns with tall palms and cypresses make a strangely Neapolitan setting for the English cottage, but the colourful flower beds, planted terracotta urns and Madeira pebbled paths make for a harmonious union. To the left, the Estate offices, somewhat decayed in a diminution of purpose, nonetheless convey the pastoral charm that characterises this garden. Ahead, a slowly declining walk follows a stream lined with flowers and leads to the centre of the garden.

Appropriately this focal point is occupied by the chapel built by the first count. From here, almost hidden amongst the vigorous vegetation can be seen the windows

LEFT The topiary hens, one the best-loved features of today's garden, replaced a knot garden of golden box originally planted by Mildred Blandy in the 1950s.

of the Casa Velha. It is said that this view from the count's house enabled him to assist at the Mass, comfortably seated in his dining room. Planted around the chapel are some of the most important camellias brought in by Mildred Blandy from China in the 1960s.

The Long Walk leads away from the chapel flanked by what are to all intents and purposes double herbaceous borders. The planting delights in kaleidoscopic colour. Although criticised by many visitors educated in the received school of Jekyllian tone, the effect is delightfully carefree. Intense modern combination, perhaps serendipitous, can be found amongst the innocence of this cottage garden. As for the botanist, the contents of the borders can be quite perplexing.

Through rose arches the walk leads on to a clutch of topiary hens that form the centre-piece of the Jardim da Senhora. This is another time warp, difficult to place. Thoroughly 1890s are the grass paths edged with blood-red iresine, the calceolaria and cineraria bedding, and also the plumbing that waters them. Yet the great rarity of many of the specimens speaks of contemporary plantsmanship and the exuberance of colour is again quite shockingly state-of-the-art. It is the most intensely visited part of the garden and leads conveniently to the Tea House.

Sneaking around the back and into the shrubberies the calm peace of indolence can once again be discovered. Here surrounding the count's house are magnificent centenarian trees: araucarias, metrosideros, liriodendrons. These narrow paths lead past the glasshouses to what is called prosaically 'The Main Garden'. This was laid out at the time of the construction of the Blandy House. Plainly geometric it contrasts with the naturalistic surroundings. Spacious with generous lawns and large trees, the crossing walks contain a large part of the Australasian and South African flora for which the gardens are justly famous. On the whole these are sun-loving species that need an open atmosphere. Indeed the proteas and banksias are prone to give up the ghost if not rattled by a good wind once in awhile. One of the rarest trees in the garden is to be found here, *Saurauia nepalensis* from Burma.

The special part of this garden, designated 'The Sunken Garden', was built as a surprise birthday gift for Mildred Blandy. As well as the South African bulbs listed above, this intimate space contains many succulents: little gems that would otherwise be lost amongst the vastness. The quirky statues and obscene topiary are amusing.

An area of the garden that is often missed by visitors is discreetly signed as the Ribeiro de Inferno. Dante's Hell contained no such prehistoric denizens; this is more like a Jurassic Park. In a deep ravine full of Madeira's tertiary vegetation, there is a furious assemblage of tree ferns, lianas of *Monstera deliciosa* and other lush vegetation that nonetheless provides a cool retreat and monochrome respite for jaded eyes.

On the way out Carvalhal's great collection of 10,000 camellia trees lines the walkway. Too tired to count them we will take his word for it.

PREVIOUS PAGE The Long Walk leads down from the chapel to the Jardim da Senhora.

LEFT Bright contrasting colours from the Jardim da Senhora in the Blandy Gardens.

ABOVE A pleasant contrast of peaceful lawns and pools with the crowded borders above.

2. Botanic Gardens

The botanic gardens of Funchal are for many tourists the gardens of Madeira, over 300,000 visit them annually. Fortunately not all at once, and the gardens which extend over fifteen hectares are rarely crowded. This is an impressive figure for a small island and demonstrates the wide appeal of flowers and gardens to both the general public, and the island tourist.

Founded in 1881 as the Quinta Reid (hotelier William Reid's country home), much of the garden today has the appeal and appearance of a private estate. The main house is traditionally built in a classical Portuguese style painted white with strongly contrasting black basalt window-frames, its trappings of colonial architecture (wooden blinds, shutters and fine-columned long veranda) are all dark green – a sober scheme that contrasts strongly with the bright and extravagant garden that surrounds it. Around the house are many large mature trees, including a magnificent English oak certainly planted by Reid. Beneath this oak, as though to set the scene for further botanical juxtaposition, is tended a diverse collection of South American bromeliads: The garden's middle altitude position (between 250 and 350 metres) enables a huge range of plants to be grown cheek by jowl – with some amusing results.

Inside the house there is a remarkable collection of Madeira natural history founded in 1882 by Father Ernest Schmitz, a German ornithologist. Within glass cabinets, beetles, snails and eggshells surround turtles and dog sharks swimming incongruously across the shining parquet of William Reid's drawing room. It is easily dismissed as macabre and out-dated. Though unfashionable, it is an exquisite period piece and could figure in any museum historian's collection.

RIGHT The many-coloured display of the Choreographic Garden is the centrepiece of the Botanic Gardens.

ABOVE Flourishing flora of the Madeira littoral: wild flowers from the kingdom of the dragon tree.

RIGHT An exercise in biodiversity: three continents and three habitats in one spot, Mexican *Agave attenuata*, Egyptian *Cyperus papyrus* and the Tasmanian tree fern *Dicksonia antarctica*.

Nowadays the important collections are alive: seed banks are held in the laboratory and the garden holds an almost complete *ex-situ* inventory of the Madeira endemic flora, together with specimens from an inaccessible rocky cliff area in which grows a tiny relic forest of Madeira woods. In accordance with modern botanic garden philosophy part of the native plantings are assembled in communities that represent the different ecosystems of the Madeira Islands: coastal plain, mountain forest (*laurisilva*) and upland plateau.

Given the difficulty of establishing plants from the cloud forests at lower altitudes the *laurisilva* plants are grouped together under the shade of the large trees that surround the main house. Having similar environmental requirements, this is where the open-air orchid collection also makes itself at home: cymbidiums, dendrobiums, sobralias....

From the mountain cloud forests the outstanding plants are those herbaceous plants that display 'gigantism' a peculiar aspect of insular endemism or what are called in New Zealand 'megaherbs'. Growing isolated from predators – in this case – herbivores, a plant can just go on evolving to get bigger and bigger. This is what happened to the giant sow thistle (*Sonchus fruticosus*), *Isoplexis sceptrum* (a sort of shrubby foxglove) and the Pride of Madeira (*Echium candicans*), a relative of the common and much smaller English wild flower viper's bugloss. In this part of the garden there is also a tree-sized spurge called locally *Figueira do Inferno*, 'Hell's fig tree' (*Euphorbia mellifera*) and a massive fuzz of green candyfloss that is a

giant climbing asparagus (*Asparagus umbellatus* ssp. *lowei*). More delicious greenery comes from the *Alegre-campo* (literally, 'joy of the field'), *Ruscus streptophyllus* and *Smilax pendulina*.

The Madeira geraniums find a home here too, both *Geranium maderense* and *G. palmatum*. These are wholly garden-worthy plants, but since this is a scientific collection there is also a cherished bindweed, *Convolvulus massonii*, and a host of other 'weeds' found nowhere else in the world and in precious few other Madeira gardens, for example: *Monizia edulis*, *Bystropogon punctatus* and *Phyllis nobla*.

Above this display is a fantastic group of Livistona palms and beyond that an arboretum, but very few visitors will make the climb, so much is beckoning from below and in Madeira one quickly learns to economise on gaining altitude. In fact this garden is most conveniently arranged with an entrance at the top and an exit at the bottom.

For the more energetic these upward paths reveal a Gondwanaland of primitive trees: Australasian gymnosperms such as *Araucaria heterophylla* and *Agathis robusta* mixed with local species of Madeira's cloud forests, vinhatico and til with Asian ginkgo and South American rubber trees and kapok. Needless to say these are plantings left over from the quinta's previous life.

On the level, long walks and terraces contain an outstanding variety of well-labelled subtropical ornamental plants. This area is a concession from the botanists for the gardener's delight. A small grotto covered with a century's worth

of accumulated moss and liverworts is presided over by an amazing oversized fern, *Angiopteris evecta*. This is also known as the giant elephant fern, a name that should give some idea of its proportions.

In these beds, rather condescendingly called the 'non-specialised collection' can be found some of Madeira's most astounding garden plants. The dombeyas, for example. Imagine a tree covered in hydrangea-style pink pompoms. Or *Schotia brachypetala*, with picturesque willow-pattern habit and bunches of red flowers like upside-down fuchsias. Fire tree, *Bracychiton acerifolius*, needs no further description.

Coming out into the sunshine a water garden fills the next terrace. The vegetation here is particularly exuberant. Great clumps of papyrus jostle for space with water hyacinths (*Eichornia crassipes*) and water lettuce as big as cabbages (*Pistia*). As a backdrop there is a curtain of ruddy volcanic stone walls studded with black *Aeonium*

'Schwarzkopf' and the massive silvery stars of *Agave attenuata* (artfully concealing the public convenience).

Further still a café terrace. How nice it is to sit and take a sip of wine in the midst of a real garden, rather than in the commercially-packaged 'museum garden' where normally one is funnelled into the tea house at the end of the trail and as a prelude to the gift shop and car park. Incidentally, there is a little shop at the botanic garden, but it is extremely well hidden and it is difficult to persuade the gardeners that staff it to part with the plants supposedly on sale.

From here one can pause to look out at the city of Funchal from the crow's nest *miradouros* above this terrace. Clinging tightly to the cliff below are remnants of Madeira's great primeval forest. The bay laurel (whose twigs are used to flavour skewered meat) is a species unique to the Atlantic Islands, *Laurus novocanariensis*.

ABOVE Spirals and cones in the topiary garden illustrate man's transient domination over nature.

RIGHT The succulent gardens: a more threatening view of nature red in tooth and claw.

Other Macronesian species found here include: the barbusano (*Apollonias barbujana*) and *Myrica faya* which Hawaiians call 'Fire tree' since it invades their volcanic slopes, and by coincidence sounds rather like the way Portuguese immigrants pronounce their vernacular name '*Faya*'. Also found, though in fewer numbers, the marmulano (*Sideroxylon mirmulans*), and a holly, (*Ilex canariensis*). Dragon trees, practically extinct in the wild landscape, have been reintroduced to this reserve.

The Botanic Garden's calling card that appears on every picture postcard is the splendidly misnamed 'Choreographic Garden'. This is a wide and spacious terrace below the café devoted to the domination and torment of coloured-leaved plants, a massive painted palette of red (*Iresine herbstii*, bloodleaf) and yellow (*Iresine herbstii* 'Aureo-reticulata', chicken's gizzard) — sounds appetising, doesn't it? There is no accounting for taste, for this is one of the most popular features of the garden. However, one can but admire the aching backs and sore knees that have produced it.

More vegetable molestation is to be found in the topiary garden, esteemed by locals as the acme of the island gardener's art: spirals, spheres, pyramids, cones and all sorts of animal effigies are to be found on display. More successful regimentation is to be found in the massed displays of carpet bedding using succulent plants, simply hundreds of the cherished black 'Schwarzkopf' *Aeonium arboreum* var. *atropurpureum* dancing with a troupe of sugary pink *Echeveria* 'Ballerina'.

The rest of the succulent garden is a tour de force. Quite literally: BE CAREFUL! The difficulties of maintaining such vicious inmates are apparent not only from the weeds that shelter under the spines, but also from the fantastic spiders' webs

spun between the arms of the cactus. No gardener can get close. But the collection is really one of the highlights of the garden, unfortunately very sparsely labelled. Some of the more easily recognised inhabitants are: *Cereus peruvianus*, descriptively called the wax candle (very tall), the mother-in-law's cushion (*Echinocactus grusonii*), old man cactus (*Cephalocereus senilis*, grey-haired), and the prickly pear (*Opuntia ficus-indica*). Others leave the visitor guessing...*Cleistocactus*, *Echinopsis*, *Mammilaria*, *Pachycereus* or *Trichocereus*?

Succulents (those without spines) are a greatly under-used class of garden plant. Water-saving and labour-free they are also colourful and of sculptural figure. Unfortunately, as in this garden, they are usually relegated to formless groups. They are in fact ideal candidates for planting design, permitting still-life composition and textural weaving. In this climate most other kinds of plant simply grow out of place so quickly that many good effects are in fact serendipitous. Plenty of good candidates for the succulent garden are displayed here, particularly species of *Aloë*: *arborescens*, *ciliaris*, *excelsa*, *ferox*; along with members of the Crassulaceae: *Cotyledon*, *Graptophyllum*, *Kalanchöe* and *Sedum*; and the Aizoaceae: *Aptenia*, *Drosanthemum*, *Glottiphyllum* and *Lampranthus*.

After the menace of the cactus and the frivolity of the carpet bedding, the economic botany section reminds one that this is a serious educational facility. The display includes every imaginable fruit, vegetable or fibre that is to be found in hot countries. From the agriculture of the island come sweet potatoes, yams and chayote (*Sechium edule*). Fruit trees are infinitely varied: avocados, custard apples, papayas, pitangas (*Eugenia uniflora*), guavas, mangos and the inexplicably baptised *tomateiro-inglês* or English tomato (*Solanum betaceum*). And of course bananas – a lot of bananas. Sugar cane was once an important cash crop on the island.

Today some is still grown to still into lethal rum called *Poncha*. The more gentle Madeira wine is also represented by some of the principal grape varieties: Negra-mole, Malvasia, Boal, Sercial and Verdelho. Cotton, sisal, and flax stand in for the fibres and olives, peanuts and castor-bean for the oils.

When the new highway was built from Funchal to the airport a few years ago, the garden was divided by a cut and cover tunnel. Far from destroying the garden this has provided space on top of the road for whole new collections, including the habitat plantings already mentioned and also big groups of palms and cycads. In a landscape that could be used as a filmset for *The Lost World*, the botanic garden has recently amassed *Cycas, Zamia, Encephalartos, Macrozamia, Dioon* in a collection that, whilst not in the same league as José Berardo's astonishing hillside of cycads at his garden at Monte Palace (pp.76–85), is very diverse and will grow up to be quite impressive. A lot of patience is required where cycads are concerned and when resources are limited.

The palm collection does suffer from indigestion: a surfeit of good things. Too many notes. One day someone will have to make a skilful edit. Palms can look tremendous when planted together in close proximity, if they are kept to single species groups. Unfortunately here they have been jumbled together and stuffed into far too small an area. There are some really interesting and fine plants: *Bismarckia nobilis, Chambeyronia rubra, Caryota mitis, Hyophorbe lagenicaulis*. But given the overcrowding, sooner or later some of the others will have to go.

For something completely different: at the bottom of the garden, the botanic theme is subverted to embrace ornithology. The Louro Parque has a flock of 500 parrots, macaws and cockatoos, 60 different species in all. As befits a botanical garden, some of the flights are beautifully landscaped, especially those of the macaws.

ABOVE AND BELOW Angels
guide wine merchants to
salvation from among the
palms and flowers of this
earthly paradise.

3. Burial Ground and English Church

Two shillings and sixpence levied on each barrel of Madeira wine built one of the most beautiful of all British overseas churches. Ten thousand pounds were raised, including subscriptions from the Kings of England and Belgium, the Duke of Wellington and other worthies. The small Anglican community chose Henry Veitch (1782–1857), Scottish wine merchant and Consul General as their architect. No doubt he chose himself. Veitch was a larger-than-life figure who later (1815) became infamous for entertaining Napoleon on his way to exile in Saint Helena. Besides the church, Veitch built many other houses throughout Madeira: allegedly to accommodate his many lovers. He is buried in his garden at Jardim da Serra, next to his favourite dog.

Non-Catholic churches were prohibited in Portugal. The law was relaxed by 1810, but nonetheless church buildings were to bear no outward resemblance to a place of worship, the use of bell-towers was specifically barred and everything was to be enclosed within high walls and a locked gate. Land was bought in 1813 and construction began in 1816. Veitch chose to build in austere Palladian style. The domed interior is wondrous. A large all-seeing-eye and cryptic symbols leave one guessing if this is a Masonic temple. The Ionic capitals of columns carved in basalt and mosaics of palms and lilies are especially fine. In a typically theatrical gesture Veitch is reputed to have placed the gold coins he received from the emperor under the foundation stone of his new church.

Holy Trinity still stands in a high-walled enclosure, though today the gate is wide open to all. The garden contains many mature trees, some of them Madeira endemics such as the til (*Ocotea foetens*) and *Juniperus cedrus*. The flora of Madeira owes a considerable debt to this garden, for many years under the care of the Rev. Richard Thomas Lowe who wrote the first Flora of the island published in 1868.

The best opportunity to enjoy the garden is following the Sunday service as the chaplain hosts a tea party. Tassel trees, tree ferns and old-fashioned roses go extremely well with a glass of Madeira wine and a chat with local church members.

The garden is currently under redevelopment, after passing through a period of difficult times. Plans are underway for a garden theatre set within wings of tropical foliage, and a chapel bower for quiet thought. The high walls are to be clothed with flowering climbers in liturgical colours: green in abundance for Ordinary Time, violet bougainvilleas for Advent and Lent, white stephanotis for Christmas and Easter and red bignonias for Feast Days.

BELOW In a gesture of floral
symbolism that the Victorian
occupants would have
appreciated, this Ionic
cross is surrounded by
everlasting flowers.

BOTTOM Celestial blue
agapanthus provide an
appropriate setting for
a cloud of white crosses.

Just a few hundred metres from the church is the Burial Ground. First established in 1765 and variously added to or subtracted from since, it obviated the need for the burial of non-Catholics at sea. As is so often the case in southern European countries, the Burial Ground stands in contrast to the surrounding old town as an oasis of green and contains, in addition to the usual assemblage of heavenly angels and forlornly-wreathed crosses, some fine botanical monuments (including the biggest royal palms on the island). Two magnificent pedimented arches proclaim, with a certain pomposity, the entrances to this foreign field 'that is for ever England'.

4. Choupana Hills

Filipe Santos, a medical doctor with a musical bent, commissioned me to design this garden with a simple analogy. 'Your gardens at the village hotel', he said, 'are like Mozart, full of fine variation. For this garden I want big themes: give me Beethoven!'

Certainly the site allowed for expansive treatment. High above Funchal with superb views over the entire bay and the wide Atlantic horizon, it occupies some seventeen hectares of steep green hillside. The property had originally belonged to William Reid and was covered with abandoned citrus orchards and brambles. Lately though it had been used as a scrap yard.

First of the 'Designer hotels' to be built in Madeira, the architectural project was created by Michel de Camaret, with interiors by Didier Lefort. The 'bungalows' are all built on pillars like Malayan long houses. Wide oriental-looking balconies seem to hover in mid-air over the precipitous slopes that form the gardens.

These steep banks are covered with great drifts of planting, acres of wild-growing ornamental grasses with perennials and flowering shrubs: hydrangea, wigandia, callistemon, lavenders and pelargoniums. In the swirling mists that sometimes cover these hills ferns of all kinds thrive; in particular one of the tree ferns, *Cyathea cooperi*. Other foliage plants predominate in the lower reaches of planting: bamboos, cordyline, gunnera and phormium.

The entrance area around the main buildings has masses of camellias with more hydrangeas and tree ferns, familiar enough treatments for a Madeira quinta. But the high retaining walls required to sustain these principal buildings have been clothed with something rather more unusual, a rampageous climber from New Zealand, *Muehlenbeckia complexa*. This vine makes a strong opening statement, falling as it does the full height of the 15 metre walls. Further down the Asian decorative theme of the buildings is developed in the gardens surrounding the swimming pool and spa. They are particularly beautiful as the sun sets over the ocean.

TOP LEFT A bright clarion of reflected light is formed by the huge clumps of New Zealand flax amongst the dark reflections of surrounding woodland.

BOTTOM LEFT An extensive vista of dissonant forms leads to a pool-side pavilion.

TOP LEFT Wide
verandas and
shallow-pitched
roofs make the
bungalows appear
to float above
the abundant
vegetation of tree
ferns and other
foliage plants.

BOTTOM LEFT
Tall cannas strike a
chord in this sonata
of green and yellow.

5. Dragon Tree Sanctuary

ABOVE A small cottage houses an information centre for Madeira Natural Park Service. It is surrounded by a garden of native plants and commands a splendid view of Funchal Bay.

RIGHT This stately clump of dragon trees and surrounding garden gives some idea of the vegetation that once covered the southern slopes of the island.

Hieronymus Bosch looking for a model to depict as the 'Tree of Life' in his *Garden of Earthly Delights*, chose the fantastical *Dracaena draco* or dragon tree. A tree dripping with reptilian blood – far better than the traditional apple. Where on earth, in 1503, could Bosch have seen such a tree? Art historians and botanists have puzzled over this: these dragon trees grow only on Madeira and the Canary Islands. The answer lies in a large tree that was recorded as growing at the Convent of the Holy Trinity at Lisbon in 1494, seventy-five years after the discovery of Madeira. The dragon tree shown by Bosch would have been just about this age since each ramification signifies some fifteen years growth.

The dragon trees growing at the sanctuary are centenarians. But like Bosch's tree they will have been planted through human intervention. Just a single tree remains growing in a wild state on Madeira. The dragon tree is almost a dodo.

Exploitation of the dragon's blood sap was not the cause of its demise. The resin could be sold to apothecaries all over Europe and was also used as a dyeing agent and varnish. But it was harvested from live trees, why kill the goose that lays the golden eggs? The end was much more ignominious, the chronicler Gaspar Frutuoso tells us the tree was good for making wooden spoons.

The garden of the dragon trees serves today as headquarters for the Madeira Natural Park. Many other native plants can be seen growing there, particularly those of the coastal forests once dominated by these trees. One splendid companion is a shrubby spurge, *Euphorbia piscatoria*. It is known locally as the *Figueira do Inferno* (fig tree from Hell). It is the food plant of a local death's-head hawk moth. What a pity Bosch didn't know about this one.

6. Ecological Park

In 1918 the city of Funchal decided to enclose a large tract of common land in order to protect the watershed that provided its citizens with fresh water. Historically the mountainside had been used for grazing cattle and sheep, but 170 hectares were sown with pines, eucalyptus and acacia in 1946. These forests were later abandoned and the rest of the 1,000 hectare reserve became infested by these invasive species.

It was not a propitious beginning for an ecological park. The first actions of the *Parque Ecologico de Funchal* after it was founded in 1994 were directed at the control of grazing and elimination of eucalyptus and acacia in order to re-establish a natural cover of *laurisilva* forest. This work continues slowly but surely. It is a Herculean task. Only in 2006 was it possible to completely eliminate grazing animals from the area. With typical self-deprecating humour the volunteer organisation that runs part of the reserve set up a business called '*A passo de Burro*' (At a donkey's pace) to provide schoolchildren and tourists with donkey rides through the park. Since 2001 the *Associação dos Amigos do Parque Ecologico* (Friends of the Ecological Park) has planted over six hectares of bare rocky mountainside with indigenous plants and each month volunteer crews maintain this young forest.

Surrounding an environmental interpretation centre and indigenous plant nursery there is an extensive garden of Madeira flora. It is easily accessible on the road from Monte to the Mountain peak of Areeiro on the way to Ribeiro Frio.

LEFT A walk in the wild mountain woodlands embellished with representatives of the island's native flora.

7. Funchal Public Garden

This is a very remarkable little garden. Indeed it is both the source and the perpetuation of Madeira garden style. Sitting at the very centre of the city of Funchal, traversed by shoppers, businessmen and tourists, it has the appearance of an 'impenetrable jungle through which 19th century explorers in sun-glasses and pith helmets should be hacking their way as in old illustrations to stories by Jules Verne.' Such was the description of Sacheverell Sitwell in 1954 and nothing has changed to belie his words.

Funchal had had a series of public promenades before the construction of this garden, but in 1880, when it was built, this was a conscious effort on the part of the municipality to modernise the layout of the old town. No less a figure than Edouard André (1840–1911), Parisian landscape architect of the Tuilleries and Buttes Chaumont, was called upon to conduct this important enterprise. His drawings for a bandstand, built in 1883 at the centre of the garden, survive in his archives. The bandstand is still with us, but has been moved to the town of Câmara de Lobos (just along the coast west of Funchal). It was dismantled in 1942 and reinstalled in the Largo 28 de Maio in 1943.

Prior to the construction of the public garden, the site had been abandoned for nearly fifty years. It had been an important monastery, the Convento de São Francisco, founded in the sixteenth century. Many travel writers and some artists depict this monastery with its *azulejo* spire and chapel of bones. In 1834 religious orders had been expelled from Portugal, and this large plot at the centre of town became municipal property in 1844. Originally the idea was to construct a courthouse and later a town hall. Neither of these projects was put into practice. In 1866 the religious buildings, including the church, were demolished. This caused much consternation amongst the local population. Perhaps the idea of a public park was first mooted simply as a measure to calm agitation, though construction only began much later in August 1880.

The original layout of the park, built as an enclosed square, can be clearly seen in old maps of the town. It contained, as well as the bandstand, a lake for swans with fountains, and numerous paisley or kidney-shaped flower beds. A block of greenhouses occupied the north-western corner next to the Scottish church. The whole was enclosed by an ornamental railing and locked up at night.

RIGHT Where else in the world do hollyhocks thrive among bananas and palms? The Funchal Public Garden is the quintessential Madeira garden.

ABOVE Looking like the source of the Orinoco, this misty garden fountain jumps straight out of the pages of Jules Verne.

RIGHT Jacaranda trees fill the city streets and gardens in April, seen here with palms, cycads and a tree fern. The red flowers are from a bottlebrush tree, *Callistemon viminalis*.

The original plants were sent from Paris by André, but subsequent plantings were obtained from Oporto, probably from the famed nurseries of Marques Loureiro, the *Real Companhia Horticola* (Royal Nursery Company). The *Gardeners' Chronicle* of 6 October 1888 illustrates the well-established gardens in a special supplement.

This garden must have spawned many others throughout Funchal, not only through the introduction and multiplication of plants, but also by training gardeners and introducing novel aspects of garden design. In 1934 when Dr Michael Grabham published his invaluable *Plants seen in Madeira* this garden was awarded a detailed twelve-page, bed-by-bed description of the plants that it contained. Three *Agathis orientalis* near to the lakes were singled out as 'erect stately trees, between 80-100 ft high…the trunks of the trees are 30-40 feet without a branch'. They scarcely seem any different today and must have grown very fast in their youth. Other such comparisons can still be made amongst the giant trees of the park.

In 1935 the avenue between the theatre and the garden was widened, occasioning the removal of the wavy railings that enclosed the park. Far from losing by the encroachment, the exuberant planting seemed to spill out onto the streets and entered a new more intimate relationship with day-to-day city life.

Today the most remarkable specimens are to be found around the edges of the garden. In the north-western corner there is a gigantuan Bella Sombra (local name for *Phytolacca dioica* meaning beautiful shade) with grossly swollen elephantine roots. Apparently unworthy of mention in 1934 this is an indication of just how fast things can grow in this climate. In the 'Jules Verne' corner around the lakes grow thick bamboos and tree ferns. Giant lianas of Swiss cheese plants (*Monstera deliciosa*) and pothos (*Epipremnum aureum)* scale the palm trunks. In front of the theatre, where it is sunny, many cottage bedding plants – stocks, petunias, candytuft and hollyhocks – are grown in company with clumps of hippeastrum and crinum. All this under frangipani and aged cycads, plus all the usual flowering trees of Funchal: jacarandas, flame trees and grevilleas.

Today the park contains 168 different species of tropical plants. It has shown considerable resistance to changing times. Despite road-widening, demolition, changing layouts, substitution of the greenhouses for public conveniences and most intrusively the construction of a covered auditorium for public concerts, it is still an essential landmark of the Funchal landscape and the pulsing heart of a garden city.

8. Hospice of the Princess Amelia

Hidden behind high stone walls and accessed from a steep flight of seventeen steps is the charitable foundation known as the Hospice of the Princess Amelia. Built in 1862 to the designs of English architect E. B. Lamb who had planned the world's first sanatorium at Bournemouth in 1855, the building is a powerful statement in carved black basalt and whitewashed walls. Originally built as a hospital for consumptives, the foundation, run by Sister Esperança of the nuns of Saint Vincent, cares for the poor through its schools, orphanages, and old people's homes.

TOP LEFT Lamb's magnificent
façade is almost totally
concealed by the exuberant
vegetation of this traditional
Madeira garden.

BOTTOM LEFT Count
the number of times the
branches of a dragon tree
fork and multiply by fifteen
to get a pretty good estimate
of the age of the tree.

The garden is contemporary with the establishment and has some glorious 145-year-old dragon trees. It is said to be possible to estimate their age according to the number of divaricated branches in the head of these monsters: fifteen years for each ramification. Counting nine or ten sets from the trunk to the last branches, the theory, at least in this case, seems to hold true.

The first pair of dragon trees is placed either side of the entrance steps and a trip to the hospice is justified just for the experience of passing under their joint canopies. Climbing to the top of the flight the garden presents itself to full view, with yet more steps ahead and the massive building hidden behind a curtain of dense trees. Under the trees, the ground shines bright red from the clipped edgings of the beefsteak variety of iresine that outline every flower bed. The paths are made from tiny round beach pebbles set in elaborate patterns.

Princess Maria Amelia died from tuberculosis at the Quinta das Angustias in 1853 (just across the road from the hospice and now known as Quinta Vigia – see p. 143). The hospice was founded in her memory by her heartbroken mother, the Empress of Brazil. In 1873 the patronage of the foundation passed to her sister Josephine, Queen of Sweden, and the Swedish royal family has retained this role ever since. Their coat of arms is picked out in white pebbles on the main terrace.

There are some spectacular trees in this garden. During the summer months the flamboyant (*Delonix regia*) captures all attention. This tropical tree is rarely seen in Madeira for a number of reasons: the voracious roots destroy all pavements in their path, making it unsuitable as street planting; it needs plenty of space as it is wide-spreading and critically it is very particular about how it is watered. On top of that it can take fifteen or twenty years before it deigns to flower. But, even so, it is well worth the wait and all the hassle: the flamboyant is well named and one of the most beautiful flowering trees in the world.

An enormous kauri pine (*Agathis robusta*), is unhappily placed in this garden. The view of the main façade is completely obliterated by the massive trunk. This is a classic example of an innocent dot-planting overstaying its welcome. The central flower bed, in the days when carpet bedding was de rigueur, would have called for a palm, a cannabis or castor-bean as a focal planting. At some time someone chose to plant the kauri pine. And it stayed put, growing to enormous proportions and blocking the axial view. Sometimes a courageous chainsaw is called for.

ABOVE AND BELOW Pebble
pavements are one of the
signature details of Madeira
gardens. The hospice
contains some of the finest
craftsmanship on the island.

9. Jardins do Lago

BELOW Tall cypress trees are a rare sight in Madeira gardens since local people associate them with cemeteries; when seen they are a sign that a garden was planted by a foreigner.

TOP RIGHT A bridge crosses the lake that gives its name to the quinta. From this high point there are wonderful views out over the city of Funchal and its bay.

BOTTOM RIGHT Amongst the dense vegetation and brightly coloured flowers that surround the former house is a giant dragon tree taller than the roof.

Styled as a 'botanical' hotel and set in gardens that date from the beginning of the nineteenth century, the Quinta Jardins do Lago well deserves the epithet. Once known as the Quinta da Achada, and a former summer residence of the Bishops of Funchal, the garden history of this site begins with its acquisition by William Penfold, who lived in Funchal from 1803. This family of gardeners lived at the house for three generations.

In 1845 Jane Wallas Penfold wrote a book to accompany her collection of watercolours sketched from the flowers of the garden. Her daughter, Mrs Robley, followed suit with a slimmer volume of her own production. These books are especially valuable since the brief accompanying descriptions describe how some of today's most familiar plants arrived at Madeira. It was Jane Penfold herself who introduced the *Strelitzia reginae* to island gardeners. All told, 29 beautifully coloured plates show flowers, fruits and ferns: 'the choicest botanical productions' of the quinta (see p. 18). Wordsworth himself wrote a poem as a preface:

> FAIR Lady! can I sing of flowers
> That in Madeira bloom and fade,
> who ne'er sate within their bowers,
> Nor through their sunny lawns have strayed?

Had he come the poet would have found wide lawns some two and a half hectares in extent. The garden has many old trees that date from the earliest days, such as a spreading dragon tree, jacarandas and mangos. The lake, with picturesque bridge and a kiosk overlooking the Bay of Funchal are an exceptional feature amongst the precipitous gardens of Madeira. 'Achada', the former name of the quinta, means 'flattened' and refers to the spacious level ground on which it is constructed.

The flat surfaces are certainly appreciated by Colombo, a giant Galapagos tortoise, who lumbers around in search of botanical morsels for lunch. He arrived at the quinta some fifty years ago, carried in a traveller's pocket; nowadays he must weigh a hundredweight.

Converted to a luxury hotel in 2000 the gardens are enjoying a new lease of life under the loving care of the hotel manager Sr Duarte Silva who has introduced many new collections of plants, including bromeliads, cycads and palms.

10. Madeira Magic

Madeira Magic, opened in 2006, is one of the island's newest gardens. It is located at Ponta da Cruz, a high promontory that marks the western limit of the Bay of Funchal, at the southernmost point of Madeira. 'The Point of the Cross' was named for the huge wooden cross that Zarco set up at this spot to aid navigation on this wild coast. For long a desolate inaccessible cape, the surrounding waters have a grim history of shipwrecks, pirates and smugglers. In the nineteenth century the point became an industrial area, firstly producing salt and then a plant for tuna canning, finally, through most of the twentieth century, it was used as the town rubbish dump.

Gardens are a wonderful way of clearing up waste land. In the 1980s and 1990s, as Funchal developed rapidly towards the west, Ponta da Cruz was designated as a green area and the municipality organised a public competition for the recuperation of the site. Along the cliff top a seaside promenade was built linking the city to the beaches at Praia Formosa in the west. Gardens were planted all along the coast. The rocky cape had become a beauty spot. Extraordinary climatic conditions, perhaps the hottest and sunniest on the island, mean that the garden at Madeira Magic is the most colourful and exuberant of Funchal, with a year-round floral calendar.

Black basalt is the raw material from which this garden was made. Massive columnar rocks form abrupt retaining walls, dry stone walls form sinuous curves that mimic the natural contours of the site, and angular shards were used to make cobbled pavements. Local craftsmen worked for nearly a year piecing together all this stone. Sustainability is a buzzword often heard, but all too often misapplied. Here all materials came from the excavation of surrounding building projects, avoiding the transport of thousands of tons of rock to the island's limited landfills.

My idea was to build a model of the Madeira landscape. Over centuries agriculture has terraced the steep slopes of the island, superimposing distinctive man-made forms on the wild volcanic topography of ash cones and deep ravines. The garden has adopted these forms and shapes to create a varied and surprising circuit. The labyrinthine design has enabled the creation of distinct garden areas without resort to enclosure. As a result Madeira Magic seems many times its real size.

The garden has a story: Madeira, once an untouched wilderness, evolved as a cultural landscape through nearly 600 years, firstly through changing patterns of land use and agriculture, and then through the gradual acclimatisation of

garden plants from six continents. This story is used to lead children from local schools through the garden in order to learn about their natural environment. In an increasingly urban society they are surprised to see how things that they take for granted were introduced to the island by early settlers, and how much Madeira has changed over the centuries.

The trail begins in a newly planted natural forest: the trees of the *laurisilva* and coastal woodlands. The original trees of Madeira were cut down or burnt by settlers to be replaced by crops of wheat; early settlers had to guarantee their sustenance or starve. A small wheat field is sown alongside twice a year. Once settlers were sufficiently established they looked for a cash crop. Sugar cane was brought from Sicily in the sixteenth century and was grown so successfully that Portugal was able to flood the European market. The price of sugar fell by half as a result, and Funchal became the wealthiest town in Portugal. The city still displays five sugar loaves on its coat of arms as a token of those glorious times. The plot of sugar cane provides visitors with an opportunity to see, *and taste*, sugar in the raw.

The next area of the garden is composed of a network of vines suspended on chestnut poles. This represents the cultivation of wine grapes for which Madeira is famous. During the eighteenth and nineteenth centuries the local economy was entirely based upon the export of wine. Underneath the vines local vegetables are grown: yams, sweet potatoes, gourds and even cabbages. Vines are still an important crop but, especially at lower altitudes, they have been supplanted by bananas. The trail ends in a grove of *Musa* 'Dwarf Cavendish', the sweet little banana that is so much more delicious than those that reach English supermarkets.

Among the bananas there is a pink Wendy house – or so it would appear. In fact this is another traditional element of the Madeira landscape: the *Casinha de Prazer*. All town gardens of Funchal had a 'House of Pleasure' from which female members of aristocratic families could observe passing society. These belvederes provided diversion from cloistered lives, and also relief from summer heat. Madeira's smallest museum is displayed inside: an exhibition of surviving examples of this colonial architecture. Alongside there is a bubbling spring that feeds a *levada* or water channel, another unmistakable element of the man-made landscape of Madeira. It flows along the boundary of the garden to a lily pond.

From this point onwards the garden is divided into large areas dedicated to

Madeira's global flora from different continents: Europe, Africa, North and South America, Asia and Australia. Plants from over the world have been continuously introduced to the island, firstly by the settlers, then by explorers, later by foreign merchants and lately by returning emigrants. Many of these plants thrive so widely on the island that even local residents cannot be convinced that they have not always grown on the island. A good example is *Strelitzia reginae*, emblem of the Madeira Tourist Board. This plant was discovered in South Africa by Francis Masson and first grown by Sir Joseph Banks at Kew in 1773, it did not reach Madeira until introduced by Mrs Penfold in the nineteenth century (see Jardins do Lago, p.62).

The flowers of Europe are those of the cottage garden, aromatic herbs predominate: lavenders, myrtle, rosemary and sage. Stately acanthus emerge from thickets of box and oleander with periwinkle trailing at their feet. This garden is spectacular during the late winter and early spring months, principally due to the colours of biennial flowers: stocks, snapdragons, foxgloves, columbines and sweet williams. These have always been favourites with the Madeira gardener.

The cottage garden look has persisted from the earliest gardens made by English wine merchants. It is the juxtaposition of these homely flowers with tropical exotics that makes the public gardens of Funchal so surprising.

Africa occupies an altogether larger area. Principally it is the flowers of the Cape that blaze with colour year-round. A long bed that accompanies the *levada* is composed of strelitzia and other plants that share its outlandish colour scheme: blue agapanthus and plumbago, orange tecomaria and leonotis. On the other side of the path are masses of succulent plants: lampranthus, kalanchoe, aloe, euphorbia. Diversity of form takes precedence over colour. The other senses are not forgotten either. Big trees of *Kalanchoe beharensis* are irresistibly touchable – the velvet plant – but the plant is so tough it seems to take any amount of fondling. The triangle palm from Madagascar (*Dypsis decaryi*) is wreathed with stephanotis whose thick white jasmine-like flowers provide year-round fragrance. A coffee plantation loaded with berries promises taste as well as the fruits of tamarind (still a young tree). And hearing? Well you have to listen very carefully to hear the sesame pods pop.

Glorious African daisies are found throughout Madeira. Arctotis form wide clumps of silver leaves, there are yellow, orange, red, pink, purple and white varieties. A similar range of colours is found in gazania, these flower throughout the year. Osteospermum, in an ever increasing range of new hybrids are becoming very popular. The florists' gerbera, a fussy plant to grow, seems to do very well in the hot dry conditions at Madeira Magic. More elegant is the Jamestown daisy, the original species, *Gerbera jamesonii*.

South America is closely linked to Madeira through the large numbers of islanders who now live in Venezuela and Brazil. Consequently there is an enormous variety of plants from this continent found growing on every porch and doorstep. Some of these plants, such as the fuchsia and the heliotrope were among the earliest garden plants introduced to Madeira. Later arrivals such as the bromeliads are much loved and seen everywhere. In this garden a dry stone wall, two metres high and fifty metres long, is filled with these and other South American epiphytes. Passionflowers are another plant that locals are convinced has always grown on the island. The squash made from its fruits is divine.

Moving north the American continent has provided very few plants to Madeira gardens, however from Central America up into California there is a host of cacti, agaves and other spiky horrids that are an indispensable component of the Madeira garden. A *miradouro* in the form of a volcanic cone rises in the centre of the garden. It is here amongst the rocks that all these lovelies are cultivated out of harm's way. There is an exquisite contrast between these muscular plants with the annual flowers that sow themselves amongst them: cosmos with purple opuntias, salvia and tagetes with steely-blue agaves, and eschscholtzia with striped furcraeas.

A spiral path climbs to the summit of the peak, from where there is a 360 degree view of the entire garden and wide ocean horizon. It comes as quite a relief after all the close-quarter looking, sniffing and touching of plants.

Where next? Asia? Asian plants abound on Madeira. Some areas practically seem so well colonised by bamboos and camphor trees that one could expect a tiger at any moment. But here on this rugged cape growing Asiatic plants is a little problematic, this is not exactly Singapore. The problem was solved by bringing in the Anzacs. Nothing thrives in hot, exposed WINDY conditions so well as the Antipodean phormium, hebe, cordyline, araucaria, coprosma, melaleuca, metrosideros…the list is endless. All these plants were planted in the front line, between the ocean storms and the garden. They take quite a battering (seven storms in their first winter) and shelter the rest of the garden in their lee.

Back to Asia. A deep pit with concentric circular terraces was constructed from basaltic rocks, at the centre a lotus pond. Sheltered by the walls and surrounding hedges are pink ti-plants (*Cordyline fruticosa*, pronounced as 'tea' but not related), and Japanese azaleas, Black Dragon ophiopogons, and bright yellow carex and acorus, multi-coloured crotons (*Codiaeum variegatum* var. *pictum*) and a multitude of alocasias – elephant ears. Amazingly all this thrives with very little damage. Only the *Nelumbium* refuses to flourish. Something wrong with the Zen?

There are other features in the garden besides the global garden. Large areas are devoted to the coastal flora of Madeira, including perhaps the largest single planting on the island of *Echium nervosum* (Pride of Madeira). Dozens of dragon trees, too, are slowly making their presence felt. Visit the tea house hidden at the bottom of the garden; you'll need a break after such a long journey.

11. *Miramar*

BELOW The old Miramar hotel was incorporated into the new Pestana Miramar. Tropical plants evocative of a traditional Madeira garden were planted at its front.

RIGHT This garden is an outdoor hothouse with brilliant coloured foliage and lavish floral display all year round.

The old Miramar was part of the Funchal social calendar. 'The Cabin', a long low building that stood between the elegant colonial hotel building and its annexe, was home to a small orchestra and a terrace bar from which locals and tourists alike would dance out into the gardens until 'quite late'. Frances Roper, a middle-aged pharmacist staying at the hotel in September 1954, complained to her diary of both the music and the cicadas 'which simply screamed all night'. The Miramar was a favourite destination for such gentlefolk, looking to avoid the expensive hotels such as Reid's and the Savoy. It offered many of the same advantages: magnificent views over the Bay of Funchal, exemplary Madeira hospitality and was only a few minutes walk from the Casino, the Lido swimming baths, and, best of all, was right next door to the British Country Club (Quinta Magnolia, see pp. 108–19).

ABOVE Familiar houseplants such as peace lilies and goosefoot vines grow as groundcover under cycads and dracaenas in a garden designed along traditional island lines.

RIGHT Luxuriant bold foliage of philodendrons and the variegated *Dracaena fragrans* 'Massangeana' contrast with the paler foliage of dragon trees and giant strelitzia.

In Mrs Roper's journal, published online by her nephew, there are photographs of the garden showing extensive grounds filled with banana trees and cannas. There were wide surrounding lawns with mature trees: jacaranda, the Madeira til, Norfolk Island pine and large hibiscus bushes. Next to the hotel was a wide-spreading parasol of *Cupressus lusitanica*, trained over a pergola under which afternoon tea was served.

With the disappearance of scheduled shipping lines, such as the MS *Venus* which had brought Mrs Roper to Madeira, the traditional hotels gradually disappeared. Not only the Miramar, but also the Miles Carmo, the Monte Carlo, Monte Palace and so many others. All gave way to luxurious modern buildings served by the new airliners and a new type of tourist to whom the quaint charm of these inexpensive guesthouses seemed old-fashioned and uncomfortable.

For many years the Miramar stood abandoned. Its gardens were built over with warehouses and workshops, and the wide lawns disappeared under road improvements as Funchal grew to the west.

In 2000 a new hotel was built in a horseshoe arch surrounding the preserved colonial-style building. Working with the architect David Sinclair, my brief was to incorporate the surviving features within the new garden design. Some fine old trees remained: Madeira til, a carob, *Grevillea robusta* and the rain tree (*Samanea saman*). Big clumps of the massive green-and-yellow-striped bamboo (*Phyllostachys bambusoides* 'Castillonis') and a fully mature Peruvian pepper tree (*Schinus molle*) were transplanted to new areas to make way for the drive. A huge camphor tree

(*Cinnamomum camphora*), which once spread out over the dancing terrace had nearly died, but happily it has responded to better care and watering.

Such is the luxuriance of the gardens that, despite the greatly increased volume of building, the new hotel is practically invisible from the street. Behind high iron railings, miraculous survivors of the road-widening scheme, tall queen palms and banyans (*Ficus benghalensis*) jostle for position with kentias and dracaenas. The domed canopy of the huge rain tree shades a garden designed to emulate traditional Madeira garden style. Paths are constructed from red volcanic tuff and clinker, a small bridge is made from rustic work in tree heather, and baskets of orchids and ferns hang from the low overhanging branches, which also sport all kinds of bromeliads. Many of the plants of this garden are familiar to overseas visitors as house plants. Calatheas, marantas, *Spathiphyllum wallisii* (the peace lily, what a marvellous piece of marketing was that common name!), peperomias, philodendrons and pileas, to name just a few. Mother-in-law's tongues stand to sharp attention lining the paths, their rigid form making a welcome contrast to the frenzied foliage of multi-coloured crotons, striped pineapples and blood-red iresine.

A quiet green calm may be found in a fern court that serves as a stairway, the walls lined four storeys high with a curtain of *Monstera deliciosa*. Giant tree ferns shade the cool walk, whilst the balustrade is draped with *Goniophlebium subauriculatum*, a south-east Asian fern that has been adopted by Madeira gardeners as their own. Gentle mist irrigation keeps the cicadas at bay. Mrs Roper would have been grateful.

12. Monte Palace

A most extraordinary garden, where East meets West, North blends with South; an Aladdin's cave of wonders, peopled by a multitude of sculpted figures; a curious cabinet of garden art that unconsciously mimics Alexander Pope and the Tradescants. This is a garden that cares not for artificial propriety, but seeks to dazzle and amaze.

Another of Madeira's garden palimpsests, the Monte Palace garden has a long history. The remnants of previous garden makers are ever present, as is the hand of Mother Nature, to whom the site belongs. Gardens are ephemeral beings, and never more so than in the pungent presence of the force of a native flora barely controlled. At present Nature and Art are held in uneasy equilibrium. When the present garden was established, in the mid-eighties, Nature was banished, and the garden had an awkward, troubled expression. Today, despite the never-ending accumulation of good things, Nature has regained the upper hand and the tension is in her favour.

It is then, a collector's garden. For here, the collection is of collections: there are animal, vegetable and mineral. And it is difficult to say which is the finest. Each visitor will be appalled and delighted at every turn, for this is one man's fantasy, and there is no accounting for taste.

That man is José Berardo. A fortune made from South African gold has made this former emigrant one of Portugal's wealthiest citizens. Returning to his Madeira homeland he established a foundation that has its headquarters in a garden. The charitable works fostered by the institution are largely concerned with the well-being of local people, but the personal interests of the founder have created a garden that is unique and suggestive.

A long time ago this land belonged to the Jesuit Fathers of Funchal. Upon the confiscation of their assets in 1760, their holdings at Monte were put up for auction. By 1773, after passing through the hands of Francis Theodor, the land of which the present-day garden forms part was sold to the British Consul of the day, Charles Murray, who built his Quinta Belmonte. Later under different ownership it became known as Quinta Prazer. *Prazer* means here a pleasance or pleasure ground in the same way that the summer houses of Madeira are known as Casinhas de Prazer (literally houses of pleasure). It was Murray who built the *levada* that brings water to the garden, but only in 1900 was the house now known as Monte Palace built by Alfredo Guilherme Rodrigues (1861–1942). Rodrigues is said to have been inspired by the castles of the Rhine for the design of his mansion or alternatively by his visit

BELOW Modern planting and
pieces from José Berardo's
fantastic collections surround
elements of this historic
garden to tremendous effect.

to the Paris Exhibition of 1900. But in fact the design is scarcely quixotic; rather it is a typical Swiss cottage or chalet, if rather large for the genre.

The house was indeed exaggeratedly large for a private residence, and the source of financial embarrassment for its builder. Quickly it was transformed into an hotel (opened 21 March 1904). It was described as having 'a magnificent park of about fifteen hectares, tree-lined walks, gardens, springs and a lake with cascades, "water chutes" and boating'. The hotel functioned until the Second World War when the property entered a period of decline.

The year 1987 saw the property sold to José Berardo. The following year it was transferred to his new charitable foundation. Work on the garden began in earnest following a campaign to eradicate the forest of invasive species that had overrun the estate. Remarkably a significant population of native woodland had survived the onslaught, including the virtually extinct mocano (*Pittosporum coriaceum*), junipers (including some centenarian specimens, *Juniperus cedrus* subsp. *Maderensis*), til (*Ocotea foetens*), bay laurel (*Laurus novocanariensis*) and barbusano (*Apollonias barbujana*). Based upon these survivors a significant part of the garden (5 hectares) was devoted to the re-establishment of the mountain forest habitat that once covered these mountains. This work was carried out in 1990 under the direction of a young geography teacher, Raimundo Quintal, nowadays acknowledged as the doyen of Madeira flora.

The garden was opened to the public on 5 October 1991 and today receives over 200,000 visitors a year. The Berardo Foundation also organises school trips from all over Madeira, so that the young of the island have an opportunity to understand the natural world around them.

The exuberant plant life of the park makes for a bewildering experience; this is a garden that needs to be explored with a map, for without such a guide many features will be missed. Even so objects loom as though out of a thick mist, constantly surprising on every turn of the labyrinthine paths. The steep terrain makes for an energetic walk.

Generally the garden is entered at the top (near the cable car terminus), where recently were planted a pair of olives said to be a thousand years old (or is it two thousand?). They were brought from mainland Portugal following the construction of a massive dam. Despite the fact that there is a native species of wild olive, the production of olives and oil is unknown on the island, since the climate is unsuitable. These giants are kept healthy on a strict regime of pesticides.

LEFT The house though large is dwarfed by massive vegetation. The garden is fed by constant humidity that promotes ferns and mosses on every surface.

BELOW There are ornamental fowl and fishes everywhere. Here a peacock strikes a pose rivalling the many sculptures that surround the house.

RIGHT A matchless collection of South African cycads fills an entire valley. Fruiting specimens are frequent. The plants are well labelled and cared for impeccably.

FAR RIGHT This rocky cascade makes for a slippery pathway around the aquatic fortress but supports a lively colony of chain ferns, maidenhair and selaginella.

BELOW *Geranium palmatum*, one of the three endemic species of Madeira cranesbill grows freely in this garden.

FAR RIGHT BELOW *Fuchsia corymbiflora* from Andean cloud forests grows as though it were a wild plant in these permanently drenched conditions.

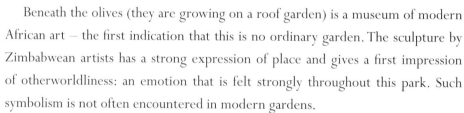

Beneath the olives (they are growing on a roof garden) is a museum of modern African art – the first indication that this is no ordinary garden. The sculpture by Zimbabwean artists has a strong expression of place and gives a first impression of otherworldliness: an emotion that is felt strongly throughout this park. Such symbolism is not often encountered in modern gardens.

An underworld (a modern grotto of sparkling rocks) is to be found in the crypt of this museum. The exhibition is entitled 'Mother Nature's Secrets'. Who was the last garden maker to collect spar and flints? Certainly no one in the last 200 years.

Emerging once again to the light, the first part of the garden to be visited is the ecological forest. Much of the tree planting is still very young, but this has the advantage of admitting dappled sunlight to the forest floor allowing many flowering plants to thrive. Madeira natives such as the Pride of Madeira, *Echium candicans*, cranesbill (*Geranium maderense*) and daisy (*Argyranthemum pinnatifidium*) provide an impressive show of local colour. This is Madeira. Here, momentarily at least, the garden is securely located in the present time and place.

Entering the garden proper, an entire hillside is covered by gigantic cycads, well over a thousand individuals provide a most unusual prospect, wholly un-European. In fact there are representatives of all the world's families of cycads. In 1990, 297 mature specimens, belonging to 33 species of the genus *Encephalartos*, were brought from the Transvaal of South Africa. They are considered to be one of the most

important *ex-situ* cycad collections in the world. They were arranged and originally tended by South African landscape gardener Steve van Blommenstein.

One garden that has not succeeded in transporting the visitor afar is the Scottish heath garden. Thousands of heathers were planted when the garden was established, but the Madeira climate at this altitude has not accommodated the immigrants. Strangely there are areas of the high mountain plateaus of Madeira that feel exactly like Scotland. But not here.

Nearby on this hillside there are some venerable individuals swimming in a large pond. Though hardly so aged as the cycads, these Japanese koi carp are impressively large and numerous. They are displayed in an outdoor aquarium such as was once common in Victorian gardens, but today this is a device unknown outside zoos and marinas. The seemingly ordinary pond has a glass wall through which visitors can appreciate the varied colours and enormous size of the fish, who in turn stare back at the multifarious crowd that gathers at their window.

Leading on from the hillside, the woodland gardens are coloured by enormous drifts of pink azaleas beneath which orange clivias cover the ground and agapanthus proliferate, thick as bluebells in an English spring. Tree ferns are commonplace and light up the darkest corners, revelling in the constant dampness that breeds a mossy softness in velvet rocky crannies that are found throughout the garden. Suddenly an oriental theme breaks upon all this greenery in strident cinnabar red.

Painted concrete piers conduct lattice-lined walkways from one level to another, leading from a laughing Buddha's den, past solemn lion dogs amidst tall bamboos, and on to quiet pools surrounding contemplative pagodas.

Portuguese gardens are perhaps best characterised by their liberal use of *azulejos*. This is an Arab tradition that has maintained a distinctive look through the centuries. The painted tiles, originally blue and white, evolved through many styles and forms; representatives of each may be found displayed in this garden. Though displaced from their original context, the panels do add structure and movement to the long garden walks that wind through the valley. In addition to the historic collection, specially commissioned works illustrate the history of the Portuguese nation and their kings in panels a hundred metres long.

Following the walks down to the house leads one to the centre of the park and Alfredo Rodrigues's extraordinary water garden. This has been lovingly restored, and indeed improved. The water chute is still there and comic striped bathing houses (they must date from this period) remind one of the Edwardian-era hotel. But it is the aquatic fortress that catches all attention. Just what Rodrigues had in mind is baffling, but the turret bristling with cannons spouting torrents of water brings to mind some of the most theatrical of Italian gardens, such as Canzio's Villa Durazzo Palavicini. It is surrounded by grottos and arcades dripping in ferny luxuriance.

FAR LEFT China red columns work an extraordinary magic among the wealth of green foliage that would otherwise overwhelm this oriental sculpture garden.

ABOVE The railings and other vermilion details give a strong sense of place and identity to this part of the garden.

BELOW Different moods from the many faces of Buddha.

Swans patrol the lake just as they did 100 years ago, more koi nibble at their feet. Peacocks strike sculptural poses on balustrades around the house, and bands of noisy bantam scatter through the shrubberies. The wide terrace provides a welcome respite from the steepness and enclosure of other garden areas. Numerous bits and pieces are displayed here, including, apparently, the world's largest vase, a frankly hideous object.

The gardens lead on below the house, but by now there is a feeling of more is less, and only the promise of a complimentary glass of Madeira wine at the pleasant cafe bar, down at the bottom of the valley, succeeds in encouraging further exertion. In fact the effort is rewarded by huge beds of cymbidium orchids and another, rather more decorative oriental garden, built around formal pools.

By now the crowds of ornamental sculpted figures will have made themselves known. They are perhaps the most notable aspect of these gardens, not quite dominating the massive mantle of vegetation, but peeping constantly upon the conscience, disturbing the mind, insisting. Victorian maidens are embarrassed by naked fauns, who in turn must perturb the concentration of the most meditative Buddha. Portuguese peasant girls mingle with Egyptian princelings and saintly bishops. The collection is so diverse and so numerous that even a garden as complicated in form as this feels, not a little, overpopulated.

Perplexing is the question where do all these figures come from, how do they belong? Perhaps the answer is to be found in the subterranean vault behind the house. There, surrounded by display niches, lies a crystal coffin. It contains a sleeping, snow-white maiden. This is no innocent creature of fairy tale, yet she seems the muse of the place. What a story the Brothers Grimm could write around the denizens of this enchanted forest!

LEFT An aquatic fortress remains the veritable tour de force at the core of the historic garden. It has been lovingly restored.

13. Monte Public Garden

Monte is very different from Funchal. The Portuguese have dubbed it the 'Sintra' of Madeira. By this is meant that a cool, lush, greenery dominates. Just as the regal hill town of mainland Portugal provides a welcome respite from the heat of Lisbon, Monte sparkles with freshness as the subtropical summer palls.

A road was built from Funchal to these heights in 1802. The English merchants of the day fast discovered the charms of these mountain valleys. As winter tourists fled the heat to England, the likes of Charles Murray and James Gordon decamped with their families and entire households for the summer season. Many illustrious quintas were founded from this time onwards. The famous basket sleds that descend from Monte were invented as an expedient method of popping into the shipping office in Town. The rather less than commodious ascent by bullock cart was later superseded by a funicular railway. With the railway, came the riff-raff, and the private domains of privilege were replaced by popular hotels (Monte Palace Hotel, 1904, and Grand Hotel Belmonte, 1926).

The construction of the park began precisely the year that the railway arrived at Monte (1894). It took five years to build – hardly surprising considering the abrupt nature of the rocky terrain. Today it is a magnificent survivor of nineteenth-century horticulture. In an era of excess, this garden shines with the simplicity of a single concept: green. There are, of course, moments of floral indulgence: the jolly yellow giant Madeira buttercups of spring or the wash of pale blue hydrangeas through early summer; but essentially the garden is drenched in deepest verdure.

Switchback paths climb down from the twin towers of the Monte church to reach the charming fountain and square of Our Lady of the Mount with its bandstand and quaint tea houses and then fall vertiginously from sight under the high stone viaduct that used to carry the railway over the ravine. Way down at the bottom there is a *miradouro*, a difference in altitude of 80 metres from top to bottom.

The garden today divides between the upper half, which retains much period charm (for which read kitsch – how about a duck pond with a replica Madeira-shaped island made of knobbly tuff?) and the lower reaches where restoration work in the late 1990s introduced a significant amount of native flora whilst retaining the original path structure and box hedging of the traditional Madeira garden. Throughout the park are fuchsias, shrubby lobelias, daturas, magnificent tree ferns and acres of agapanthus (see p. 14).

ABOVE A scarlet flash of *Salvia sessei* mesmerises this green panorama seen from the vertiginous heights of the stone viaduct at Monte.

14. Pestana Grand

The gardens at the Pestana Grand Hotel are designed to be seen from the imposing glass lobby. From the cliff top at Ponta da Cruz there are breath-taking views over the Atlantic Ocean. The garden needed to be composed of bold elements that would frame the panorama without obscuring the wide horizon. The garden is also looked down on from the many verandas of the façade so an approach of flat patterned colour on the grass was adopted. My design is thus an abstract composition using only three species of plants: *Phoenix dactylifera*, *Pennisetum clandestinum* and *Verbena tenuisecta*.

The date palms were imported from Elche, a Spanish town near Alicante that has a palm grove classified by UNESCO World Heritage, the only one of its kind in Europe. Brought over as bare rootless trunks, and looking more like telegraph poles than trees, they took a couple of years to develop the spherical crown of leaves that today cast a graceful shade on the lawn.

The second species, *Pennisetum clandestinum* (Kikuyu grass), makes a lawn that is fresh, bright green and soft to walk on. The Grand Hotel is supplied with ample water from the *levadas*. Without sufficient water tropical lawns can be harsh and often tend to crisp to a colour that is more purple or brown than green. With much less water Kikuyu produces a lawn that rivals the best Bermuda turf. During hot summers in Madeira, when the east wind blows from the Sahara, a plague of caterpillars called 'army worms' can devour a lawn in three days. The tough rhizomes of this grass are not to their taste and these lawns quickly recover their lush appearance.

Verbena, with its soft candy pink flowers, provides the perfect contrast to the almost lime green grass. The flower beds are laid out in scrolls that give a nod to Burle Marx, but really owe more to Loudon and Paxton's Victorian 'paisley beds'. The flowers are there by popular demand. Initially the beds were planted with the rich purple foliage of *Tradescantia pallida* (better known as *Setcreasea purpurea*). But the desire to produce an abstract design appealed more to designers than to the general public.

BELOW Patterns of shade play upon the lawn beneath palms, as seen from the reception of the hotel.

BELOW LEFT AND RIGHT
Basalt rocks provide niches
for a multicoloured variety of
succulent plants.

BOTTOM A promising young
forest of dragon trees mingles
with palms and agaves.

'Where are the flowers?' they asked. And they had a point – this is Madeira, the island of flowers. And indeed over the years more flowers have crept into the design.

Another part of the same garden has a unique collection of succulent plants, growing in specially constructed basalt rock terraces. This is an introspective sheltered garden in a sunken area between buildings, quite different from the wide open space of the palm grove. The rocks are magnificent basalt shafts and columns salvaged from excavation of the hotel. They are placed side by side in ranks to form jagged retaining walls that, placed in series, resolve a tricky change in level between the hotel forecourt and the gardens. In contrast to the abstraction of the main garden these rocks house a collection of some 300 species of succulent plants: aloes, agaves and cacti. Growing amongst the cracks in the rock walls are many smaller succulent plants such as echeveria, aeonium, kalanchoe, crassula and senecio. The ground is sprinkled with the sparkling jewels of mesembryanthemum (*Lampranthus spp.*).

A grove of *Dracaena draco*, a relic of the once widespread forest of dragon trees and a strangely neglected Madeira species, has been planted on a mound. They are thriving here in their native environment; many of them have reached flowering size and will soon begin to branch out in characteristic form. They are the most impressive of the species of the Atlantic Island flora. Hopefully this small grove will contribute to their future popularity amongst Madeira gardeners.

ABOVE Patient columnar cacti lurk among the brash agaves, one day they will tower above them.

15. Pestana Village

According to an exhaustive study made by Dr Raimundo Quintal, the gardens of the Pestana Village Hotel contain no fewer than 99 families of different plants, distributed between 294 genera, 418 species, 5 subspecies, 9 varieties and 15 hybrids. Keen gardeners with an eye for cultivated plants could add a few more to that list. The garden, established in 1996, has had an enormous influence on modern gardening in Madeira. Many of its plants (newly introduced to the island) are now well established in enthusiasts' collections throughout the island.

Prior to the 1990s Madeira's garden flora had stagnated, or indeed become considerably impoverished when compared with the days of the great plantswomen such as Mildred Blandy or Theo Welsh. Collections of Australian and subtropical trees, shrubs and climbers, growing in this hotel garden have enriched the island's botanical wealth. In particular there are many flowering shrubs and perennial plants which were previously unknown on Madeira.

With Portugal's entry to the European community (1986) the island of Madeira enjoyed a period of prosperity and an explosive boom in new construction. The Pestana Village Hotel set a precedent for a new type of development in which gardens were given a leading role. Dionisio Pestana commissioned me to make this garden. After all, he argued, why do so many tourists come to Madeira if not for the flowers? The gardens have won a series of awards which have recognised the merit of this argument. Indeed many hotels built since have adopted this garden model for their layout and planning.

Growing in the former banana fields of the Quinta da Casa Branca the gardens enjoy an enviable climate where mangos and papayas thrive amongst the palms and flowers in the garden. There are frangipani trees on the lawns and roses on the walls. Tall palms and sophora shade the entrance drive. The rate of growth achieved over the first few years was phenomenal. The height that the trees and palms of this garden have attained in less than twenty years is almost unbelievable. Many of the garden's tallest trees were grown from seed. One palm, a Himalayan species (*Caryota maxima*), reached 18 metres in

LEFT Tropical planting of Madagascan palms and Hawaiian ti-plants on one of the upper lawns.

ABOVE Brightly coloured flowers fill the garden: *Canna* 'Roi Humbert' and rarely seen *Doryanthes palmeri* beneath a jacaranda tree in the top picture. Then (from left to right): *Canna* 'Wyoming', *Tecoma stans*, *Canna* 'City of Portland'.

less than ten years. *Melia azedarach* trees, planted as saplings, are now taller than the hotel buildings.

This garden was deliberately planned to provide flowers throughout the year. Many of Madeira's traditional hotel gardens were winter-flowering to coincide with what was then considered high season. Tourists hate to be told that they should have seen the garden last month when such and such trees were at their magnificent peak. By planting a garden with such a wide variety of species it is possible to overlap these moments of glory. Even during the hottest parts of summer, when most of the island's gardens are wilting, the garden is full of colour. By the same token the great majority of these summer-flowering plants are evergreen so as to provide foil for other winter splendours. According to Raimundo Quintal, there are 118 plant species in the garden that flower continuously, every month of the year.

LEFT Sunlight streams through foliage surrounding the shady entrance porch, highlighting the shocking pink leaves of *Cordyline fruticosa*.

16. Quinta do Arco

BELOW Grandiose scenery provides a spectacular setting for this breath-taking rose garden.

RIGHT A wide expanse of the Meilland hybrid rose 'La Sevillana' greets visitors to the garden.

Miguel Albuquerque is a passionate rosarian: a self-confessed compulsive collector who has amassed an enormous collection of the genus. The roses are planted in spectacular scenery, between mountains and the ocean, making for a garden that transcends the ordinary parameters of rose growing.

In such a powerful landscape Albuquerque has wisely chosen to plant a selected few of his roses in great masses. The effect of a scarlet field of flowers set against blue seas and bluer skies is breath-taking. The mountains lean down hard over the garden, making one feel small, very, very small. Just then, amidst such grandeur, a single bloom of *Rosa rubiginosa* draws minute attention and suddenly everything is turned topsy-turvy. Like Blake we are drawn to see a 'World in a Grain of Sand And a Heaven in a Wild Flower'.

The benign growing conditions of the north coast of Madeira tend to encourage the roses to somewhat outgrow themselves, and ingenious techniques must be employed to keep them within bounds. Roses are grown to good effect over hooped arches, as in classical French rose gardens, and others are tied down in bundles to create tangled flowering briars. Pyramids of *Rosa wichuraiana* hybrids, vigorous, flexible and healthy roses, produce a wonderful display. The same is true for the Tea Roses, though these are rather trickier to keep within bounds.

RIGHT Once inside the garden
there are places where even
the overbearing mountains
are excluded by the sheer
number of roses.

Reading through Albuquerque's book on old garden
roses one finds comments like, 'in warm climates this
rose easily reaches five metres in height' or 'the plant has
good foliage, strong spines and grows to considerable
size in warm regions'. All this is followed up with some
such demoralising comment as, 'in the countries of
Northern Europe, this rose has a sickly weak constitution
and can only be grown in glasshouses'.

One of the appeals of an old rose collection is the
host of fascinating personalities evoked by names
given by the early rose breeders. Cardinals and Grand
Dukes, Queens and Countesses crowd the garden.
Rosarians' wives too, are to be found in abundance.
Names like 'Mrs. Herbert Stevens' were an opportune
way for breeders to perpetuate their own names. Some
pretty unlikely juxtapositions occur: 'Fantin-Latour',
'Robert Le Diable' and the 'Village Maid' (all *Rosa
centifolia* hybrids) share a bed together. The collection
is impeccably labelled, no mean task considering all the
pruning that must be undertaken. Keeping tabs on such
an unruly mob must require the patience of a saint.

The collection now numbers some 17,000 rose
bushes and has spread from the original gardened area to
new gardens dubbed the Roseiral Duquesa de Bragança.
It seems quite appropriate that these aristocratic flowers
should enjoy royal patronage.

The Albuquerque family estate of Quinta do Arco
has been converted into a comfortable hotel with small
cottages providing rural accommodation. Many of the
areas surrounding these buildings are also gardened.
Here in addition to the roses there are also the native
flowers of the Madeira countryside: Paris daisies
(*Argyranthemum pinnatifidum*), Pride of Madeira (*Echium
candicans*), the Madeira cranesbill (*Geranium maderense*)
and the Madeira bluebell (*Autonoe madeirensis*).

17. Quinta da Boa Vista

Sir William Cooke, Bt (1872–1964), was a breeder. With an overwhelming passion he bred hunters, polo ponies, hounds, chickens, racehorses, Abyssinian cats, shorthorn cattle and orchids. Perhaps the enthusiasm began with horses, but it was with orchids that he found the allure of betting against Nature's odds most compelling. Bringing together gene pools from all over the world he was able to create artificial hybrids of greater and greater sophistication; laying the foundations for modern-day cymbidium, lycaste and paphiopedilum.

His orchids, housed in ten heated greenhouses at Wyld Court in Berkshire, formed one of the great private collections of the day. From this collection came much of the original genetic material now dispersed in the chromosomes of orchid hybrids the world over. During the Second World War these precious plants were sent to the United States. Here they provided breeding lines for the fledgling American cut-flower industry.

Today the orchids are to be found at the Quinta da Boa Vista where they form part of the collection belonging to Betty Garton (Sir William's daughter) and Patrick Garton (his grandson). It is an extraordinary thought that many of these plants are just a slip away from the wild plants collected by intrepid plant hunters of the Amazon and Himalaya. This precious wild-collected material is maintained by occasionally dividing off young plants, but many of the original plants have outlived Sir William by decades. As to the hybrids, orchid breeders are patient folk. Sometimes it is necessary to wait up to fourteen or fifteen years for seedlings to flower before rejecting all but the very best of the litter. Some of the orchid breeding lines established by Sir William in the 1920s are still undergoing development. His plants and their descendants continue to win many awards and certificates. Some of the most famous of these plants include *Lycaste* Wyld Court 'Sir William Cooke', *Wilsonara* Tigersette 'Wyld Court', and *Cymbidium* 'Blue Smoke', named appropriately enough after a racehorse. The names of many of these orchids contain the word 'Wyld' such as *Lycaste* 'Wyldfire', 'Wyld Peach' and 'Wyld Delight'.

Both Betty Garton and her father served as Orchid Committee members for the Royal Horticultural Society. The nursery that Betty established at Wyld Court won many certificates, awards and medals for its plants, including a Grand Champion Hybrid at the British Orchid Council. Patrick Garton has received a Gold Medal from the RHS for his series of watercolours illustrating orchids from the collection.

The Quinta da Boa Vista has belonged to the Garton family since the mid-nineteenth century. Group Captain Cecil Garton was an enthusiastic customer of the Wyld Court orchid nurseries and it was through this shared passion that he met and later in 1968 married Sir William's daughter. After 30 years in the RAF, Cecil Garton retired as military attaché in Lisbon and Madrid and became an Honorary British Consul in Funchal.

The quinta lies to the east of Funchal, off the old Conde de Carvalhal road. It was formerly an agricultural estate devoted to banana culture, later market garden produce was grown to supply shipping liners. The connection with flower growing was first established through the introduction of the commercial production of strelitzias: an important cash crop for Madeira before the days of airfreight. Cecil Garton and his new wife gradually turned over the entire quinta to orchids, principally to supply cut flowers to the local market and visiting tourists.

Today, in the face of fierce competition from imported cut flowers, the collection has once again become the principal interest of the family business, attracting many visitors to the garden throughout the year. In the winter months most of the flowers are provided by the cymbidiums, however there are cattleyas and paphiopedilums (slipper orchids) to provide a year-round display.

Just inside the main greenhouse there is a small shop where orchids, bulbs,

seeds and all the wonderful paraphernalia to delight an orchid devotee is offered for sale. Two shelves display plants brought from the back collections for special attention. Those on the top shelf are prized items from the private stock, whilst those on the lower shelf are offered as rare opportunities to acquire surplus plants from the collection.

Patrick Garton has developed the gardens to include a far wider range of plants, including some spectacular flowering climbers in the orchid houses. His aim is to achieve a star-performing plant display each month of the year. Three such show-stopping plants are *Thunbergia mysorensis*, *Strongylodon macrobotrys* (the jade vine) and *Aristolochia grandiflora*. Nor have the gardens surrounding the greenhouses been forgotten. Here Patrick has planted out many of the superb bromeliads that are his own special predilection. Jealous gardeners can but drool over such beauties as the enormous *Alcantarea imperialis*, as yet unflowered but going to reach three and a half metres in height. The steps leading down from a side gate frequently used as an entrance by visitors are lined with pots overflowing with aechmea, billbergia, guzmania, neoregelia and vriesia. Hanging down from the vine pergola overhead are silver chains of Spanish moss (*Tillandsia usneoides*) providing perennial surprise and glee.

The seventeenth-century house is a perfect example of the Madeira country house. It is built on simple lines with red stone window frames (*cantaria*), complete with colonial touches such as the wooden shutters and a quaint vertical oval widow with star-shaped fenestration. In front of the long regular façade there is a lawn under giant exotic trees: eucalyptus, araucaria, jacaranda, tipuana and chorisia. The frangipani flowers here sweetly throughout the summer months, surrounded by enormous Hawaiian hibiscus. In the winter months the display is largely secured by sculptural plantings of flowering aloe and euphorbia. There is a wide wooden terrace on which teas are served. It provides a platform that overlooks the spectacular view of the Funchal Bay (the '*boa vista*', good view, that gave the site its name). For many tourists a visit to this garden provides a unique opportunity to see a traditional Madeira quinta, and to enjoy contact with a family that has made its home there on the island for generations.

FACING PAGE
From top left clockwise:
Laeliocattleya THAIS DE VALEC.
Slc (Sophrolaeliocattleya) Jewel Box 'Scheherazade' AM/RHS, AOS.
Maxillaria tenuifolia.
Strongylodon macrobotrys.
Pescatoria roezlii x *Zygopetalum* John Banks.
Angraecum veitchii.

ABOVE LEFT
Neoregelia 'Passion'.

ABOVE RIGHT
Guzmania musaica.

BELOW *Aechmea tessmannii* x *chantinii.*

18. Quinta das Cruzes

Zarco (the one-eyed), discoverer of Madeira in 1419, made his home at this spot and marked it, not with an X, but a cross. The House of the Crosses is thus the noblest and oldest of all the Madeira quintas, continuously inhabited and developed for nearly 600 years. Nowadays the property performs its dignified task as principal museum for the decorative arts and is surrounded by a quixotic and intriguing garden.

To the left of the gate is a fountain amidst pretty flower beds with the characteristic pebble pavements of Funchal. A typical arrangement, and historically correct, yet somehow this public court lacks soul: it has been fatally institutionalised. Fortunately the rest of the garden, hidden away behind an archway, has survived the transition from private residence to public monument rather better. Such a difficult task. Charm has a fugitive quality, often it is in the neglected corners, where gardens can gather moss, that the magic survives …

The springs and fountains of this garden have kept it alive. Nothing grand. This is far from the wealth of metropolitan Portugal which imported marble statues from Genoa and brought back the spoils of the Orient to decorate its gardens. The materials are all local, only the plants are exotic. Volcanic stone lends a Neapolitan air, but it is used with such ease that we are firmly grounded in local custom.

Just through that arch, amidst a graveyard of architectural salvage, is a small tank enclosed in an elbow of walls encrusted with small rocks. The fountain oozes picturesque detail, and is crowned by sword ferns and dripping maidenhair. Composed architecturally of a series of consecutive arches, the structure is encrusted with knobbles of purple tuff. This rock is known on Madeira as *feijoca* or 'red beans'. It is composed of consolidated volcanic ash, just as is found around Vesuvius or Etna. There are other fountains, similarly clad, including

RIGHT A classically inspired grotto rusticated with knobbles of volcanic rock is colonised by a host of ferns and mosses.

BELOW AND RIGHT Details
from the decaying fresco of
Poseidon and Amphitrite that
adorns a small nymphaeum
in the garden.

a sadly waterless dolphin at the end of a long walk lined with walls of the same stuff. Amidst the huge orchid collection which occupies one corner of the garden there is a grotto decorated with shards of crockery (English willow pattern for the most part).

At the very top of the garden, and concealed from all but the most curious visitor, is a cascade that controlled water flowing into the garden from the *levadas* of the mountainside. Here the decoration is also based on applied tuff, but this time in geometric patterns: an eight-pointed star and various lozenges. This fountain has some architectural pretension as it sports a pediment enriched with a frieze of acanthus leaves and the water is made to tumble down a stairway to a platter sculpted in timid baroque.

The last of the waterworks is also the most intriguing: timorous gods caught fleeting from sight are captured in the flaking plaster of a decaying fresco. The trident-bearing god rides towards a naked goddess and small cupid-like child. This seems to be a representation of the triumph of Poseidon and Amphitrite, rulers of the ocean, and as such forms a befitting tribute to Zarco. Amphitrite spawned dolphins, seals and whales from this union. Zarco's family adopted the seal as their family crest.

19. Quinta Magnolia

In 1826, the fifth United States consul to Madeira, John Howard March (1791–1863) decided to build a new house, importing for the purpose a shipload of pinewood planks from Savannah, Georgia. With it there came a collection of American plants to decorate the garden. Patriotically the property was named after the finest of all eastern American trees, the magnolia.

March was a New Englander, resident in Madeira since 1810, and consul since 1816. As a wine merchant he traded with his elder brothers Charles and Thomas in New York, and had agents in Philadelphia, Savannah, Alexandria, Philadelphia and Boston. He sold Madeira wine at 20 to 30 shillings the pipe and imported goods such as fish oil, lumber, salt cod, pipe staves, corn, wheat and rice, making a gross profit of between 150 to 200 per cent. His company records are preserved at the University of New Mexico.

March lived in town on the Praça do Constituição (on the present site of the Bank of Portugal, near Zarco's statue). His house had a considerable walled garden in front, full of fruit trees. It was entered by a large door, over which there was a summer house and a balcony decorated with a painting of the American eagle. The Stars and Stripes flew at the mast on a high turret. Isabella França, a nineteenth-century diarist, described the garden's flower beds, full of beautiful plants, with a *Melia azedarach* and a double-flowered honeysuckle. Pebbled paths led to the steps up to the main door and a terrace overlooking the public walk. Isabella was startled in the evening light by a silent woman standing on the stairway. March had placed there the figurehead from the prow of one of his ships, *The Creole*, wrecked in 1842. This wooden sculpture is today in the Museum of Fine Arts in Boston.

The Magnolia, on the 'rua nova' (New Street), was in fact a mile and a half out of town. There was no real garden at this time, the greater part of the quinta was profitably planted with vines. A teetotaller known for his parsimonious lifestyle yet spending his winters in Paris and London, March is remembered in Madeira as a philanthropist. He rebuilt the church of Santo Antonio da Serra and provided famine relief when crops failed due to potato blight and phylloxera. His nephew Charles Wainwright March (1815–64), author of *Sketches and Adventures in Madeira, Portugal, and the Andalusias of Spain* (1856), inherited the quinta in 1863.

The garden as it exists today was laid out at the end of the nineteenth century by Dr Herbert Watney (1843–1932), physician at St George's Hospital, London.

RIGHT Lush tropical vegetation fills the visitor with expectation at the entrance court: cycad, *Encephalartos lehmannii*, flashes in the sunlight, surrounded by cordylines and tree ferns.

He was Master of the Mercers' Company, and Lord of the Manors of Bradfield and Ashampsted in Berkshire. But in Madeira, during the winter season, he was able to pursue his vocation as a considerable amateur horticulturist. He lived at The Magnolia, as the family affectionately referred to their island home, for over 40 years, during which time he amassed an impressive collection of plants. His particular predilection was for palms.

An album of photographs from 1898 shows the garden substantially complete. In front of the house the middle terrace was planted with flowery box parterres and surrounded by urns planted with agaves. Rather appropriately for this scion of a famous brewing family, scattered around there were half barrels, each filled with young palm trees. To one side of the house there was a tall signalling mast decked with flags. This was a feature common to all the Madeira quintas, as essential to commercial life as the social calendar was to the exiles' private life. Lawn tennis and croquet provided fashionable amusement.

Flower beds cut into the lawns and edged with coloured foliage show how the Victorian English influence continued. But the botanical interest of the garden was far superior to this. Each year Watney introduced more treasures to his garden: palms, cycads, screw-pines, dragon trees. And the more extraordinary the form, or rarer the species, the more he coveted their costly variety.

The elaborate system of cliff-hanging paths was probably laid out at this time. In addition to accessing a number of fountains and viewing platforms, these led to a large cave appropriated by the family as a cool retreat. Today this is used as a gardeners' bothy. Clearly visible in the photographs taken from the *miradouros* was the bridge built in 1849 that strode across the ravine of the Ribeiro Seco (dry river). The modern road bridge hides from view the still extant gothic arches of this bridge, just as the primitive hump-back is concealed at its feet.

Herbert Watney died in 1932. Shortly before this the property had been sold to the Blandy family, who, together with the Leacocks and other foreign merchants, founded the British Country Club as a social bastion against changing times. The garden slipped into benign neglect and accommodated gentlemanly pursuits such as a nine-hole golf course.

In 1980 the Regional Government expropriated the club as a public amenity, There ensued a rigorous building campaign, more tennis courts, a massive swimming pool (obliterating a large part of the palm collection) and squash courts dug out of the cliff-side. Surprisingly, despite the physical aggravation, the garden has since then enjoyed a period of rejuvenation.

Quinta Magnolia lives today for its remarkable vegetable denizens: six-headed hydra cycads or reclining sphinx-like dasylirions. They are the botanical testament

ABOVE These cycads
(*Encephalartos altensteinii*)
are poised to thrive for at
least another couple of
hundred years.

BELOW A centenarian
dasylirion reclines with
dignified old age.

RIGHT Herbert Watney would
be justly proud to see the
tremendous development of
the palms and cycads in his
garden; this cycad is some
five metres tall.

to a 200-year history of plantsmanship, now held in the thrall of championship
tennis and jazz festivals. And thank goodness for both! The gardens so preserved
are now one of Funchal's principal urban green spaces, surrounded by the intense
development of the last quarter of the twentieth century.

As a public park, Quinta Magnolia figures low on the garden visitor's agenda.
The entrance is, it must be admitted, uninspiring. A replacement *Magnolia grandiflora*
stands encaged within wasp-striped crash barriers amidst the four-wheel-drive
vehicles of Madeira's Civil Defence Agency (it has its headquarters at the quinta).
But perseverance has its reward. The ticket booth is there only for swimmers and
would-be tennis champions; for gardeners entrance is free and for those able to
abstract the least desirable elements the park is a delight.

The house, at least from the exterior, is in fact scarcely altered from the time of
Dr Watney, a tribute to the good taste and delicacy of the architect who made the
conversion to public use. Originally a hotel school was installed in the club. Well-
informed tourists were able to take five-course lunches sitting at wicker chairs.
Drinks were taken on the pebbled terrace amidst strutting peacocks. Domineering
supervisors hovered over trainee waiters as they struggled to open ancient vintages
from the former club's cellar. Unfortunately the club rooms now stand empty.
A most original public library, dedicated to the literature of Madeira's many visitors,
allows an opportunity to inspect the interior; but the charm has vanished, better
to press on to discover the rich menagerie of palms and cycads spread throughout
the grounds.

The entrance court gives an idea of the scale of things on offer, giant furcraeas (vividly striped relatives of the agaves) launch flower spikes five to seven metres into the air, a clump of dwarf palm trees, only three metres high, is seen on closer inspection to be but a single specimen, a multi-trunked example, of *Cycas circinalis*. Another cycad lurks at its feet; this one has ferociously spiny grey-blue leaves, *Encephalartus horridus*. Over-topping all these exotic plants is quite the biggest specimen on the island of the Madeira wild olive or Zambujeiro (*Olea europaea* spp. *maderensis*), perhaps the oldest tree in the garden. Sadly it is in marked decline.

Laid out in front of the veranda of the house is a pebbled terrace from which all the grandest views of Funchal were once beheld: over the bay to the Cabo Girão (the cape English sailors used to call the Brazen Head), out to sea to the Deserta Islands, and up to the mountains, with a glimpse of the twin towers of the Mount Church enveloped in robust forests. These views are all gone; the trees of the park have grown exceedingly, mercifully obscuring the modern construction that would otherwise dominate the vista. Ancient-looking Monterey cypress and camphor trees (*Cinnamomum camphora*) planted along the garden's main axis and a young forest of casuarinas in the ravine mitigate visual offence.

Above the house, on the site of the former croquet lawn, there are specimen palms and a wonderful *Pandanus utilis*. The screw-pine, as it is called from the spiralling insertion of the long saw-toothed leaves, is a most peculiar beast: a chimera almost. Not in the strict botanical sense, but imagine a cross between a pineapple, a yucca, a mangrove and a palm tree and perhaps you will understand. The most striking feature is the thick awkward root system that grasps the air, clawing for the ground. The stance is of a slowly moving lizard; one can feel the deliberation. Mace-like cones bristle the surface like the armature of a griffin.

Another peculiar tree, the kauri pine dominates this area. In New Zealand the huge carcasses of prehistoric trunks of agathis are dragged from swamps to provide high quality timber. Weighing 100 tons or more, they are estimated to be at least 45,000 years old. This youngster will be around for some time.

Clumps of bamboo, suitably scaled to camouflage these creatures, attract closer attention through the girth of their culms. Some, like *Phyllostachys bambusoides* 'Castillonis', are golden, painted with green stripes, others are black or a greyish blue. The recently planted *Dendrocalamus giganteus*, moved here since it outgrew its previous location, has yet to recover from the transplant. It has the potential to reach 30 metres in height.

Cycads are found throughout the garden. This is a small collection where age counts; one-hundred-year-old specimens are common here. On the croquet lawn there is a *Dioon edule*, a Mexican species whose seeds provide a flour used to make tortillas. Large as this clump is, it would only provide a half-dozen pancakes. In its own habitat this is one of the world's largest-growing cycads. Specimens can grow to 32 metres.

NEAR RIGHT Small neatly-
tended flower beds are
teeming with bright pink
bromeliads used as
groundcover in the
ravine gardens.

FACING PAGE Cottage garden
flowers such as hollyhock
form an unexpected
centrepiece to this garden
of tropical foliage and
sculptural form.

BELOW The red flowers of
Schotia brachypetala produce
a copious nectar which is
greatly appreciated by the
birds of the garden.

Further along, past island beds of scarlet salvias edged with dayglo-orange mesembryanthemum that would make William Robinson wince, are magnificent clumps of *Cycas circanalis*. This is a strangely neglected species, it should be grown more often. It is, alas, considered too ordinary by snobbish collectors. But it has one great merit: fast growth. Cycads in competition could be compared with racing snails, but give this one ideal conditions and it will provide quite impressive results in a very few years. At Quinta Magnolia, the largest specimen has six heads on thick writhing trunks. Females produce the most alluring clutches of duck-egg sized and coloured seeds that add to their reptilian allure.

The remnants of Watney's palm collection are scattered throughout the garden, an attentive observer can still count some thirty species. A tight-knit group is wedged between the public swimming pool and the tennis courts, here alone there are seven species: *Washingtonia filifera* and *W. robusta*, *Jubaea chilensis*, *Phoenix canariensis*, *Phoenix reclinata*, *Livistona chinensis* and *Caryota mitis*. For good measure two more Washingtonias have been recently jammed in between the tennis courts and two more *Livistona chinensis* and a *Raphis excelsa* next to the steps. Annoyingly the labels, though they are hammered to the trunks, are all mixed up.

Further exploration of this garden is rewarding, though it involves descending into the ravine of the Ribeiro Seco. It is rather reminiscent of those leeside gardens found on the south coast of England with steeply-set, cobbled paths and viewing platforms (*miradouros*) formed over grottos. During the craze to add public utility to

this lovely garden an exercise course was added to the cliffside garden, a hazardous and ill-advised pursuit.

The paths explore every nook of rock and lead almost to the sea amidst soft tree ferns, tall date palms and ferocious cacti. There are some charming cottages that must have been delightful accommodation for gardeners in generations past. The precipitous drops are protected with the characteristic Madeira railings formed of tree heathers gathered in the mountains. Deep down in the river bed grows a cacophony of invasive tropical plants, huge elephant ears (alocasia and xanthosoma), clumps of indian shot (*Canna indica*), the castor-oil plant, and sheets of morning glory, passionflowers and cardiospermum – all vines that threaten to engulf the island.

A rather sad spectacle is provided by the group of aviary enclosures under the forest of casuarinas. Here once-proud peacocks suffer the indignity of confinement, treading deliberately amongst squabbling chickens. Ducks and geese puddle in muddy pens. All this is in stark contrast to the wild canaries that flock in the trees above.

Climbing back towards the park, take time to explore the intricate network of pebbled paths. This is the part of the garden that has best preserved the atmosphere of a Funchal quinta. The small, neatly-tended flower beds are teeming with bromeliads and cottage garden flowers. Specimen plants such as frangipani, dragon trees and pony-tail palms (*Beaucarnea recurvata*) are found amongst drifts of hollyhocks and daisies. This is still Watney's garden. Can you imagine Berkshire with global warming?

20. Quinta do Monte

Jardins do Imperador

The history of Madeira gardens is intimately linked to that of the famous wines of the island. Just as the early shippers created a unique style of wine to meet the demands of their far-flung customers, so it was they who imported and adapted the gardening habits and tastes of a generation that even today has left its characteristic stamp on the island's gardens. The wine merchants, through their wealth and leisure, created some of the earliest country houses around which were made splendid gardens.

The most celebrated of all these houses was the Quinta do Monte, built by the Gordon family. Thomas Gordon had come to Madeira in 1758. He was from Kirkcudbright, where the head of the family was laird of Balmaghie. One of the reasons that the Gordons became so successful as shippers was that they maintained close family ties with agents in London and New York, in addition to maintaining their ancestral lands in Scotland. Many family members served with the East India Company. This cosmopolitan outlook was reflected in the lifestyle they maintained on Madeira.

In 1820 the Gordons acquired land that was to become the Quinta do Monte. The house itself was constructed in 1826 on the marriage of James David Webster Gordon to Theodosia Arabella Pollock. An unknown English architect was engaged to prepare the plans. Arabella spent a fortune on the house and garden – £30,000 according to gossip: the wine trade was thriving.

The artist Andrew Picken made a drawing of the quinta and its garden in 1837. He was a skilled lithographer and dedicated his print to Webster Gordon; later an album of views of Madeira was published with a dedication to Mrs Gordon. Picken was tutor to the family's sons. In July 1842 he was guide to a distinguished visitor, Prince Adalbert of Prussia, who was clearly impressed by the 'splendid flower-garden, containing a rich collection of rare exotics…with trees from all parts of the world…enlivening the view on every side'. European silver-leaved firs and oaks, a 'large abundance' of banksias from New Holland, and plants from North America were recorded by the prince in his journal. Picken's drawing shows clearly great clumps of arum lilies, an early introduction from South Africa.

J. D. Webster Gordon died in 1850 leaving the Monte estate to his eldest son Webster Thomas Gordon. He was a professional soldier with the 66th Berkshire Regiment, spending much of his life on active service in North America and India. Perhaps this is why he gave the quinta to his younger brother Russell Manners Gordon in 1851. Russell Manners Gordon was by now a Portuguese citizen and held

LEFT Venus endlessly wrings her long-dry hair, her foot resting on a dolphin that no longer spouts. The effect is charming enough but would be much enhanced with a little extra plumbing.

BELOW This coloured lithograph of Andrew Picken's painting of the house and garden in 1837 was made for private circulation.

RIGHT The wide terrace of
box hedges and colourful
annual flowers provides
the setting for the
Malakoff Tower.

RIGHT This fairy-tale cottage stands at the gate to the quinta. It contains a small museum of photographs illustrating the history of the house and garden.

BELOW The Malakoff Tower that was built by Manners Gordon, perhaps to celebrate the military exploits of his clansmen in the Crimea.

the noble Portuguese title of Conde de Torre Bello. An advantageous marriage had also made him the largest landowner on Madeira.

Manners Gordon made many improvements to the quinta, walling the property and constructing a formal garden terrace and turret that commanded a magnificent view of the Bay of Funchal. The Malakoff Tower (1855) commemorated the Battle of Sebastopol which ended the Crimean War. A number of garden follies of this name were built in France (after all the tower had been captured by the French), but whether Manners Gordon had more personal motives for the commemoration is unclear. Many members of the Gordon clan fought during the Crimea, but his brother was not among them. One historian, Colonel Chesney, wrote that 'England soon rang with Gordon of Gordon's Battery', referring to the heroic death of Captain Alexander Gordon and to the valiant efforts of his commanding officer 'old fireworks' Sir John William Gordon. However these were Gordons of Pitlurg, only distant relatives to those of Balmaghie. The terrace is built around a fountain of a nymph wringing her hair. The sculpture is based on *Venus Fiorenza* by Giambologna. The fountain originally symbolised the city of Florence, the city where, ironically, Major Webster Thomas Gordon died in 1879. In 1870 the quinta was sold to Peter Cossart, a partner in the wine shipping company since 1831. However Cossart died the same year and the Quinta do Monte came to his son Leland who made further addition to the gardens, building lakes, dams and rivulets.

By the end of the nineteenth century, when Leland Cossart died, the garden was justly celebrated, especially for its camellias, Australian tree ferns, eucalypts and oak and chestnut woodlands. At this stage the property was bought by a wealthy banker, Luiz da Rocha Machado, a native of the Azores. It was his grandson who, in 1922, was to offer the house as a permanent residence to the deposed Habsburg Emperor Karl Franz Josef who, only forty-two days later, died and was buried in the Monte Church. Nowadays the garden is more celebrated for this melancholy event than for its glorious history. Reinvented as the Jardins do Imperador, the gardens were restored and opened to the public in March 2004.

The entrance lodge has gingerbread bargeboards. Hansel and Gretel's cottage could not be more delicious. Shown inside, the visitor can admire a display of monochrome photographs showing the garden in its pristine heyday. But through the panes of the bay windows, another picture is seen. The view is framed by giant tree ferns, enormous clumps of pampas grass, and crowded by mega-herbs of all description: *Geranium maderense*, *Sonchus fruticosus* and *Euphorbia mellifera*. From the diminutive porch a long driveway leads away, signposted and neatly lined with blue and white agapanthus. Yet attention is quickly drawn into the deep shadows. A narrow path, cobbled in patterned shards of basalt, heads towards more inviting scenery. The fields are filled with orange and yellow *Canna indica*, and along the path, tree ferns push their way through as bold as bracken. Hydrangea and fuchsia hedges form thickets high above the head, and the fulsome scent of *Hedychium gardnerianum* (ginger lily) fills the air. Some distance on, approaching the garden proper, appear long-lost flower beds, their outlines now scarcely discernible. Each one is marked by a central group of lithe and vital cordylines within the bulging emerald box.

William Robinson would have been ecstatic. He greatly admired the gardens of Madeira: 'real gardens varied and full of beautiful colour, yet without any trace of the barren monotony of gardens at home.' Today he would enter into transports of delight. The whole place is a wild garden of exotic plants growing freely in grass and woodland. Robinson was convinced that the flower colour needed to be set in 'clouds of verdant leafage, so that monotony is rarely produced'.

The formal garden of the Malakoff Terrace is thickly planted with roses and cottage garden annuals: larkspur, daisies and pinks. Mixed in there are gladioli, fuchsias and begonias. The box hedging around the beds is dwarf, fat and unruly. The result is both chaotic and charming, a little clumsy, but nonetheless endearing. Individual beds can be lovely but the whole is missing cohesion. Venus, still wringing her hair, looks on heedlessly; she has seen many changes.

The Malakoff Tower has been restored, details of its colonial architecture have been repaired and painted in traditional colours. The sentinel cannon that once greeted guests and incoming ships is still there, and the signal mast stands high, though a little creaky. Naval flags for shippers and social engagements are no longer stored in the tower. Just as at the Quinta Magnolia this flagstaff is bare, today only Reid's maintains this tradition. But there are wicker chairs in the shade of old trees, as there must always have been. Take a seat and enjoy the Gordons' view. Too bad there's no one to bring you a gin and tonic.

21. Quinta da Palmeira

'Never did I see so magnificent a place as this Palmeira. The grounds must be immense; it seems to stand on a pile of precipitous rocks, or rather they surround it with a mighty rampart, beneath which my path wound for some part of its great circuit.'

EMILY SHORE, 1839.

The Quinta da Palmeira stands high above Funchal on a steep cliff. It belongs to the Welsh family, heirs of Harry Hinton (1857–1948), who was perhaps the most conspicuous member of the British community of his day. From 1895 until 1910 Hinton held an official government warrant for the monopoly of the production of sugar and alcohol in Madeira. He purchased the quinta in 1908.

This quinta has always been considered one of the foremost estates of the island and as early as 1851 Edward Harcourt (author of *A Sketch of Madeira*) published a long list of the cultivated plants of its exemplary gardens: 'As a fair specimen of perennial plants cultivated in a Madeira garden, may be taken the following list…furnished me by the kindness of C. Bewicke, Esq., being the produce of the garden of the Quinta da Palmeira.' Calverley Bewicke, who lived at Palmeira in the midnineteenth century, had taken a long lease on the property where he pursued his interest in natural history; he was known to Charles Darwin. The list runs to fourteen pages and contains plants from Australia, South America, Southern Africa and Asia as well as familiar garden flowers. As an example there are six species of fuchsia as well as hybrid varieties. Although the first fuchsia, *F. coccinea*, was introduced to English gardens by the nurseryman Lee of Hammersmith in the 1790s, hybrid varieties did not appear until 1837.

In 1840 an earlier visitor, an American naval officer, Robert Burts, described the garden as possessing a 'high guarded wall embracing about twenty acres of mountainside, partly terraced; paths of the dark shading laurel and cedars; intermingled with the coffee and fig, magnolia and acacia trees, and the flowers of the tropics. Here there was a game enclosure, there an arbour, here a fountain and there a tank.'

LEFT Bougainvilleas, frangipani and a palm tree, together with the blue horizon of the ocean, make up this quintessential Madeira garden view.

RIGHT A clock from the Hinton Sugar Mill in Funchal is just one of the reminders of the source of the wealth that built this quinta.

BELOW The bow-fronted façade with its iron balconies and green shuttered windows forms the entrance to the house.

When Hinton bought the property he immediately began to rebuild the house and gardens. The house grew to become as tall and imposing as its rocky site, and thus reflected the standing of its new owner. The unusual bow-fronted façade that had formed the entrance hall to the earlier house was raised to four storeys and wrought-iron balconies were extended across each row of shuttered windows. Elegant canopies that had graced the former dwelling were retained but moved up to the second floor, and a round turret was added at roof level. In effect the colonial architectural style had been modified to incorporate an important status symbol of traditional Funchal architecture called the *Avista Navios*. These were tall towers built on to Funchal town houses by which powerful mercantile houses displayed their wealth and kept an eye on incoming shipping.

Margaret Hoare in her book on the quintas of Madeira (2004) tells how the original entrance to the house was up 484 pebbled steps, ladies had to be carried up from the entrance gates in hammocks. Hinton changed all that in 1922. To allow his motor car to reach his doorstep, he had a precipitous cutting driven into the cliff, up from the Santa Luzia roadway. Today, garden visitors, of either sex, have to walk.

A new garden was developed by Hinton's second wife, Isabel Hinton, from 1928 onwards. This extends over wide terraces beyond the wide walkway that terminated the former gardens and is characterised by ubiquitous use of red-brick paving and walling that gives a Home Counties feel to the grounds. The source of these bricks, many of them stamped with London manufacturers' names, were demolitions and alterations to the great sugar factory at Torreão built by William Hinton, Harry's father, in the previous century. The rose garden and a sundial set in heart-shaped beds date from this period. Built under them is a fountain decorated with broken crockery in blue and white Reid's livery and bearing the date 1929. Tile decorations from the Lisbon workshop of Constância, found throughout the garden, were also put in place by Isabel Hinton.

ABOVE AND LEFT
A veranda built in 1929 for
the new garden made by
Isabel Hinton. It combines
traditional elements from
Madeira with a Home
Counties garden style.
The red bricks used for
paths in the lawn were
salvaged from the Hinton
Mill at Torreão.

The family name of the next generation was Welsh, as the house passed by inheritance to Hinton's stepson George in 1948. Widely travelled George Welsh was married to a New Zealander, Theo Florence Beswick. There was, it seems, a friendly rivalry between Theo and the South African Mildred Blandy in the provision of exotic planting for their gardens and once again the botanical wealth of the gardens of Quinta da Palmeira reached notable dimensions. Theo lived in the house until she died aged 93 in 1995. Naturally the gardens had declined somewhat in her old age but recently they have been adopted by her grandson Eduardo who is tackling them with vigorous enthusiasm, as indeed he does any project that he takes on. Harry would be impressed.

The garden can be divided into several spaces, each owing its creation to different periods of inspiration, though connoisseur planting from Theo Welsh can be found throughout. Behind the house is a small villa garden that may date from Harry Hinton's building but seems more in keeping with previous incarnations. Typical Madeira pebbled paths trace a complicated arrangement of box-edged flower beds, rather overwhelmed by the plants they contain. Two garden buildings, or rather a

LEFT The giant oaks that lined the Broad Walk have been gradually replaced with other types of tree. The banks are covered in white agapanthus.

loggia and a fountain placed at opposite ends of the terrace are probably from the 1920s. The fountain bears the date of 1461, but that is in homage to the epic poet Camões who is supposed to have visited the island in that year en route to the Indias. The erythrina at the back of the house, which flowers in spring, was already considered one of the largest on the island a hundred years ago.

The garden front of the main house is dominated by large trees dating from the nineteenth-century gardens. Here there was little scope for twentieth-century garden making in their dense shade and this is why the modern gardens were formed below the wide terrace known as the Broad Walk at the foot of the long diagonal path that transverses the steep banks. An enormous til (Madeira native, *Ocotea foetens*) is perhaps the most notable tree of this group. The ground under the trees, photographed by Cecil Miles in 1949 (*A Glimpse of Madeira*) covered by millions of pelargoniums, is now replete with white agapanthus. A fountain basin with two decorative urns placed in a small formal lawn and giant clumps of Gymea lily (*Doryanthes palmeri*) are relics from former times.

A line of giant oaks lined the Broad Walk, probably at least 200 years old,

but they are now gone or in marked decline. The horticultural highlight of this terrace is a huge vine, *Combretum paniculatum*, which blooms a vivid orange (in the first half of the year) above the tiled seat overlooking the Caminho da Torrinha. It is unique on the island.

The garden below occupies the formerly agricultural terraces of the lower *fazenda* (farm). Here Isabel Hinton laid out an axial arrangement of steps and walks. It begins with a sentimental heart-shaped flower bed and a sundial and progresses down through semicircular steps and small pools to end with a very pretty grotto of broken crockery set beneath a viewing platform. It reminds one of illustrations from Country Life books such as *Garden Making by Example* (G. C. Taylor, 1932) that offered advice to numerous home county garden-makers in the period between the two world wars. Pergolas are planted with bougainvilleas and the stairways enlaced with wisteria. The flower beds are full of geraniums, roses, chrysanthemums, lilies, pansies, petunias…just as they would have been in the 1930s. The views over the Bay of Funchal are superb. A croquet lawn is surrounded by low walls covered in interesting plants, in particular the brilliant blue *Petrea volubilis*.

It is here that the tall date palm that gives it name to the estate is growing, surrounded by Italian cypress. When Palmeira was visited in 1909 by Florence Du Cane, she noted the 'incredible beauty' of the stone pines and cypresses of the quinta, and lamented the fact that this was the only villa of Funchal that could 'boast the possession of fine cypresses'. The situation with regard to these trees in Madeira remains much the same, for the Portuguese feel they belong only in cemeteries.

Beyond the cypresses are smaller terraces with ancient irrigation tanks and a platform that holds the chief monument of the garden, famed as Colombus's window. Harry Hinton obtained the window on the demolition (1877) of the house of Jeanin Esmeraut (João Esmeraldo), a Flemish merchant who arrived in Madeira around 1480. Columbus first visited Madeira in 1478 to purchase sugar for the Genoese merchant house of Centurione. The following year, in Lisbon, Columbus married Filipa Moniz, daughter of Bartolomeo Perestrello (1395–1457), captain of Porto Santo. In 1498 he made a brief visit to Madeira during his third voyage to the Americas. The evidence that Columbus may have lived in this house is extremely thin, but tradition is enduring.

LEFT The tall date palm that gives its name to the Quinta da Palmeira grows on the lower terraces of the estate. The semicircular steps are once again built from bricks salvaged from the sugar factory.

22. Quinta Pestana

'An English-garden, with a big lawn, a walk all around the boundary and not too many exotic-looking plants'. Such was my client's succinct brief in 1991. The house, low-roofed with wide verandas on a butterfly plan, was under construction. Built in the former *fazenda* of the Quinta da Casa Branca the most striking feature of the building's large plot was a long cobbled driveway leading from impressive iron gates. But it ended in a blank wall of concrete blocks, hastily erected to divide the building site from the gardens of the former owners.

Though the site certainly had its capabilities, the negative aspect of its present condition was somewhat overwhelming. At the bottom there was a busy main road. There was also a massive concrete wall erected in a space that had been expropriated by the municipality to allow for road widening at some future date. Between this wall and the new house was a huge hole destined to be an underground office block. The remaining spaces were full of dead plants: the trees of the avenue sickened with honey fungus and the bananas of the farm dying of drought.

But this was a wonderful site: nearly three hectares in the centre of Funchal, just across the street from Reid's Hotel. Surrounding it are some of the best of the island's residential quintas, originally built by English wine merchants. There was plenty of *levada* water (a reservoir holding 1,000 cubic metres was to be built to supply the garden) and the climate was simply enviable.

The house belonged to Dionisio Pestana, a successful young businessman and hotelier. His wife had grown up in Sintra, a Portuguese town famous for its gardens. They wanted something of this romantic atmosphere, a softer feel than the luxurious subtropical gardens of Madeira. The garden was begun in 1993.

LEFT The garden is built around two large lawns. The upper lawn is an octagon terrace closely integrated with the butterfly-shaped form of the house.

In the meantime plans for the office block were abandoned and a circular lawn, 50 metres in diameter was sculpted in its place. The bottom of the lawn was dug down to street level so that the concrete wall built for the road-widening would provide an effective sound barrier. On the eastern boundary a high retaining wall was also built and a 100 metre long pergola walk ran along this limit. Initially it was planned for the house to give out onto a series of flights of steps to give access to the lower lawn; however this idea was set aside in favour of a broad octagonal terrace. A double staircase and balustrade then led down to the lawn. The pergola walk continued along the top of the roadside wall to pass over an old stone bridge that was inherited from the garden's former incarnation as part of the Quinta da Casa Branca. From here an informal path led back to the house while the perimeter walk led on to an area dedicated to a nursery and orchards, tennis courts and the swimming-pool house.

Decorative features for the garden were made by the English artist John O'Connor. In particular there are four large tile panels, for, despite the brief, this is a Portuguese garden too. The panels display a certain whimsy that was designed to appeal to the Pestanas' young growing family: there are Kipling-like monkeys

playing in a fountain and frogs that could have jumped out of the pages of *The Wind in the Willows*. The largest of the panels shows a *trompe l'oeil* view of the Bay of Funchal which could be mistaken for Naples.

Today, after fifteen years of development under the devoted care of its English head gardener Derrick Hill, the garden has a look of maturity far beyond its youth. Trees have grown to astonishing heights: *Acrocarpus fraxinifolia* grew some twenty metres in half a dozen years, a large group of hoary *Ficus rubiginosa* look as though they are fifty or more years old, and a 'Bela Sombra' (*Phytolacca dioica*) threatens to rival the ancient-looking specimen that grows at the corner of the Funchal Public Garden.

Disregarding the brief, a number of palms were planted in an ordered structural pattern that now punctuates the garden's spaces. These have now reached mature dimensions. In particular the tall elegant columns of the Alexandra palm (*Archontophoenix alexandrae*) placed around the points of the octagonal terrace reinforce the architectural quality of the geometric space.

Flowering trees and climbers were selected to give the garden a year-round display. Many of the trees are common favourites of the island such as spathodea, erythrina, grevillea and jacaranda, but there are others more rarely seen such as

LEFT A tile panel painted by John O'Connor blends an imaginary view of Funchal Bay with the columns and vines of the pergola walk.

ABOVE This informal walk passes through dense vegetation that has grown to astonishing dimensions in a very short time.

tabebuia, calodendron, radermachera and bolusanthus. One of the most splendid climbers is *Beaumontia grandiflora*; another not grown on the island elsewhere is the bright orange *Juanulloa aurantiaca*. A huge *Solandra maxima* pours out from the pergola onto the street causing astonished tourists to grab for their cameras when it flowers through the winter.

The garden was planned to incorporate a very diverse collection of plants but was carefully ordered by flower colour. The long sloping pergola begins with red bougainvilleas that blend with dark blue plumbagos and then pale thunbergias, which progress on to pink *Antigonon leptopus* and white jasmines. There are large wide mixed beds that more resemble meadows than herbaceous borders. The largest, on either side of the double stairway, are planted respectively in gorgeous reds, oranges, yellows and purple blues and indigo. The plants are Australian, African, Mexican and Brazilian, but there are enough simple daisies and roses, iris and lilies to maintain a cottage garden feel despite the exotic palette. There are large collections of salvias and plectranthus, vireya rhododendrons, penstemons and daylilies.

At the focal point of the garden's main axis there is a semicircular pond at the foot of a rocky cascade. A contemporary Danish sculpture of a young woman is barely visible within the recesses of a dripping cave behind curtains of ferns, lilies and reeds. Frogs sit on the lotus pads croaking at their companions on the tile panels.

Visitors to the garden are always astonished as they cross the cobbled drive at the side of the house. This roadway, heavily planted with traditional (and exotic) Madeira garden plants such as huge aloes, cycads and strelitzia leads to an entirely unexpected second half of the garden, ostensibly devoted to leisure activities such as the swimming pool and tennis court, but also packed with many interesting plants. These have been accumulated through years of plant collecting but simply have not found their place in the main gardens. There is a large shade house and nursery that supplies the garden with fresh plantings; an allée of Judas trees under-planted with arum lilies that is a homage to Sintra gardens; a rose-covered colonnade and vine trellises; thick woodlands of Madeira til planted as screen planting and a long secondary driveway lined with palms carpeted with red salvias and hosts of *Alocasia* 'Black Magic'.

ABOVE The pergola walk sustains many different types of flowering climbers, bougainvilleas, thunbergias, wisterias and bignonias but the overall effect is of radiant verdure and relaxation.

23. Quinta de Santo Antonio

BELOW AND RIGHT Two views
of the farmland or *fazenda*
that surrounds the garden.
Vines and bananas still
provide an income for
the estate.

One of the oldest houses in Funchal, the Quinta de Santo Antonio is believed to date from the fifteenth century. During these 500 years it has remained in the possession of the same family, descendants of Bartolomeu Perestrelo (*c.*1396–1457), Captain of Porto Santo Island. The current owner Mary Goodley, a great-granddaughter of the Visconde de Ribeira Brava (Francisco Correia Herédia), inherited the property from her mother Maria Ana Rootham.

The quinta was originally used by the family as a summer house and referred to as the 'Casa da Vindima' (vintage house) as it was used for the harvesting of grapes. Beneath the present house the bottom half of the building was devoted to an *adega* (wine cellar) in which barrels were stored to be sent down to the town house in the Rua Queimada de Baixo. As well as the Malvasia (Malmsey) grapes, there were pine woods for buildings and firewood, sugar cane to be sent to the mills, and fruit and vegetables. Cows were kept in quaint A-framed sheds to provide fresh milk.

The house was extended in the nineteenth century to provide more spacious accommodation in the summer months. It was at this time that a garden was laid out, as indicated by the date 1871 set into the pebbles of a terrace overlooking Funchal Bay.

Today the quinta retains this arrangement of house and garden (flowers, fruit and vegetables) surrounded by a *fazenda* (agricultural land) and *mata* (woods). This was the model for island self-sufficiency and is a pattern that has all but disappeared from the modern landscape of Madeira. Today the principal commercial crop is bananas, though some grapes are still grown.

The garden is a delight and the personal creation of Mary Goodley, who has lived at the quinta since the outbreak of the Second World War. Born in Pernambuco, Brazil, where her father was employed by the Atlantic Cable Company, she arrived in Madeira from South America on 2 September 1939. The ship on which she had arrived was torpedoed as it left Madeira and many of its passengers lost their lives. On that voyage her mother had brought with her a pot of bougainvillea that still grows over a pergola that forms a little summer house. Remarkably it produces kaleidoscopic flowers that change colour as they age from white to pink and red and even orange.

As with any long inhabited space, every corner has a story to tell. Mary Goodley's progress is slow; these memories come flooding back as she walks

through the garden. Hanging from the dragon tree there are terracotta bowls with perforated sides. They are specially constructed for the cultivation of a fabulous vanilla scented orchid (*Stanhopea tigrina*) that pushes its flowers out through the base of the pot. 'Stanhope, you see, was a friend of the family…a frequent visitor to the island.' At the bottom of the garden is the '*rondinho*' that must once have been the threshing floor. 'This is where the family would take their tea…over there is the path where the servants would come down from the house… see how it is hidden behind that tall hedge.' Out of Mary's earshot her husband John Goodley tells his own story of how he almost set a tall oak tree alight with a rather enthusiastic bonfire.

Although also a repository of traditional Madeira garden plants, the native flora of the island has always been championed in this garden. There are sheets of Madeira geraniums (*Geranium maderense*) under the oak trees and clumps of the rare Madeira bluebell (*Autonoe madeirensis*) border a lawn. The Pride of Madeira and Madeira daisies (*Argyranthemum pinnatifidum*) grow on the hillsides bordering the *fazenda*, while the walls of the vineyard bristle with *Aeonium glutinosum* (among South African aloes).

Stroll a little beyond the garden and you will find the old Madeira. A landscape hand-carved from the hillside: dry stone walls, *levada* channels that provide water to the terraces, vine pergolas, a track to the pine woods. Only the inhabitants of the cow shed have changed. The occupants now are the luckiest tourists on the whole island.

24. Quinta Vigia

A tiny chapel dedicated to Our Lady of Sorrows was founded on the cliffs above the Bay of Funchal in 1662. The quinta to which it lent its name, the Quinta das Angustias was built in the eighteenth century by a formidable woman, Guiomar Madelena Acciaoli, and later Nicolau Hemitério de la Tuellière incorporated the chapel into the main building. This superbly-sited property is now the home of the president of the regional government. Anyone can just walk in. There is no pomp, and the most discreet security; the garden of the presidential palace is one of the best kept secrets of Funchal.

Not surprisingly the regional government changed the name when the property was bought as the official residence. The new name, Quinta Vigia, was taken from an adjoining house that had been demolished to make way for Brazilian architect Oscar Niemeyer's project at the Casino Park. This could be translated as the Watch Tower or Look Out. In fact one of the most striking features of this garden is the Mirante de Dona Guiomar. An eighteenth-century garden folly (built between 1766 and 1775), it surveys the most magnificent view over the harbour and Bay of Funchal, as far as the cape known to English navigators as the Brazen Head. Out to sea, on fine days, the Desertas Islands are clearly visible.

LEFT The cross gives a clue to the chapel, now incorporated into the main building; inside the interior is covered with devotional paintings.

BELOW The garden is laid out with box-edged compartments divided by cobbled paths, but there is no formality as the beds are filled with a hectic mixture of plants.

The chapel still bears the psalmist's lament '*Tribulatio et angustia invenerunt me*' (Trouble and anguish have found me, Psalm 119:143) above the doorway. Scenes of the Seven Sorrows of Mary line the walls and the Instruments of Christ's Suffering decorate the ceiling. The altarpiece shows the Virgin Mary standing at the foot of the cross, her heart graphically pierced by a huge sword.

Trouble and anguish have indeed found some of the previous occupants of this house. In 1846 the Misses Rutherford, wealthy tenants of the house, were attacked by an angry mob led by clergy from the cathedral as they sheltered protestant converts and the house was almost burnt to the ground. In 1853 the twenty-two-year-old Princess Maria Amelia (daughter of the former Emperor of Brazil) died here after a short struggle with tuberculosis. Her grieving mother founded the hospice named after her in her memory on land just across the street (see pp.60–61).

The gardens that surround the house and chapel were considerably remade by the regional government between 1979 and 1982, but they reflect the traditional taste for Madeira gardens and would delight J. C. Loudon in his quaintest Victorian mood. Individual flower beds are defined by dwarf walls encrusted with knobbles

FAR LEFT Bromeliads, tree ferns, palms, cycads, orchids, crotons and conifers: these are the stuff of the Madeira garden.

LEFT A single plant of the native Madeira cranesbill, *Geranium maderense*, fills the foreground of this view.

BELOW One of the most impressive plants in this garden is the bamboo orchid: *Sobralia macrantha*.

of red volcanic stone, cages built as oriental fantasies contain brightly coloured parrots and a wiggly stream flows down to lakes peopled by soppy cherubs. The grounds are maintained by staff from the Botanic Garden and, as befits their calling, are in exemplary order.

Mass plantings fill individual beds. One of the most impressive is a large swathe of lilac-coloured *Sobralia macrantha*. These are terrestrial orchids with flowers that resemble the flamboyant cattleyas found on matronly bosoms. Sometimes called the bamboo orchid, the flowers are borne atop narrow canes at about waist height. To see them planted as though they were dahlias is a humbling experience for any gardener.

Several areas are dedicated to the indigenous plants of Madeira, demonstrating their potential as decorative ornamentals. There are enviably large drifts of the *Geranium maderense* and a huge clump of the red-flowered *Teucrium heterophyllum*, a plant that is hardly ever seen in gardens and even rarer in the wild state. A thriving community of *Lavandula pinnata* makes up for their absence at the Botanic Garden. This species was thought to be extinct on the island until a single plant was found by the late Dr Graham Quinn. As he was a long gangly man and had to hang down from the high cliffs below the Pico fortress to reach it, that particular bit of modern plant exploration must have been a comical sight. It is good to see the descendants thriving and be reminded of a much-missed friend.

The Madeira penchant for bromeliads is here indulged to the maximum, both as groundcover in the shade of ancient trees and wired to extravagant displays of driftwood. There are many species here that are simply not available commercially in Europe and this reflects the ties that Madeira has with South America through emigration to Brazil and Venezuela. In the same area of the garden are colourful carpet beds of tightly clipped iresine and althenanthera, another enduring passion of the traditional gardener. This garden has the charming effect of the undesigned. A work of naïve art that results from the purest love of plants that is proper to the island temperament.

BELOW AND RIGHT The garden is peopled by an amusing assortment of sculpture: soppy cherubs, pouting satyrs and overburdened mermaids.

25. Reid's Palace Hotel

Somewhere along the plush corridors of the Reid's Palace Hotel, there is a glass case with a magazine cutting, sepia with age. It is a picture from *The Sketch* from 1932 and shows a graceful figure, frozen by the camera, in mid-air above a sparkling ocean. The caption reads: 'Lady Prudence Jellicoe in mid-air swallow dive.' Playground for the privileged throughout the thirties and fifties the whole place retains an atmosphere of those leisured times. Much of the glamour was derived from Madeira's unique position as an accessible paradise in an age before the jet plane.

The gardens of the hotel have preserved the traditional style of Madeira gardening through the generations of horticulturally-minded general managers and owners. Once the strict preserve of the rich and famous, they have now become democratised through the institution of afternoon tea and guided garden tours. But the privilege of an evening stroll through this floating garden, as the sun sets over the ocean, is still reserved for those fortunate enough to stay as guests.

The rocky headland, stuck with palms and Norfolk Island pines, is now just a glimpse of glorious garden days gone by. But there is still a tremendous presence. Some gardens owe everything to their location: this is an extraordinary spot. Without the exotic vegetation that clothes the rocks, the site would still make a dramatic impression, but somehow, lost within the dense covering of foliage fostered by an almost tropical microclimate, the visitor is transported far away in the imagination, and it comes as somewhat of a shock eventually to emerge on a pretty terrace and be confronted by views of seemingly conventional landscape.

RIGHT The gardens of the Reid's Palace Hotel occupy an entire rocky headland.

LEFT A vital mass of exotic vegetation occupies the foreground of views over the Funchal harbour and town.

William Reid, when he bought this craggy site, had a canny eye for its potential. The world-class hotel he created has survived for more than a century. Part of his vision was to exploit the reputation of Madeira as a tropical paradise. But conditions on the rough, exposed headland were all but propitious for gardening.

Reid was a determined man. Way out of town, at the end of the only (bad) road, the garden was hauled in by teams of ox sleds. Men with wicker baskets on their backs carried the soil to fill terraces behind basalt walls. Walks were carved out from the cliffs and then painstakingly paved with tiny pebbles. Huge reservoirs were constructed halfway up surrounding hillsides to supply a constant supply of water at a good pressure.

The garden structure was thus established from the outset. The headland south below the hotel was levelled to form three broad platforms descending to a long broad walk that connected to the steeply terraced garden areas to the east. To the west, where the sea cuts sharply in to form a rocky cove, the garden takes the form of a narrow cliff top path with views out over the ocean. North of the hotel, an entrance court was enclosed by pillared gates and iron railings.

The earliest photographs show a simple layout of lawns and Canary Island palms with beds of banded agaves – robust plantings to withstand the heavy storms that frequently batter this coast in winter. From this period date the tallest araucarias and probably the majestic beaucarneas at the entrance court. As shelter developed more

ambitious schemes followed and the garden took on its present-day luxuriance.

Many of the fabulous plants in this garden are a legacy from the time when the hotel belonged to the Blandy family. A botanical synergy with the Palheiro gardens was formed by Mildred Blandy. Plants that she brought in from all over the world would be tried out in both gardens. A sort of horticultural Venn diagram developed, since very few plants would thrive in both gardens due to the great difference in altitude. So there were three sets of plants: high altitude cool-growers, sea-level tropicals, and those tolerant plants that would cope equally with both conditions.

The jade vine, familiar to British gardeners as a denizen of the palm house at Kew, is one such survivor from Mrs Blandy's plantings. Native to steamy Philippine forests it has no business growing here out of doors. Each year, in late spring, the luminous chains of flowers, looking like a Halloween version of wisteria, gleam into the dark tunnel of a gloomy pergola. It is hard to imagine a more spectacular effect. The red jade vine, *Mucuna bennettii* sent by Graham Quinn (when a young student working in Nigeria), was also cultivated here, but has long since disappeared.

An old specimen of the tassel tree (*Dombeya cacuminum*), only recently replaced by its young substitute, was another gift from a friend of Mildred Blandy. This came from Madagascar and was brought in by the husband of Simone Chazal of Quinta da Cova. The tassels are extravagant pompoms of sugar-ice pink petals fringed with pollen like gold dust, an extraordinary sight. The demise of the old tree has opened

ABOVE AND LEFT
A tremendous mixture of sculptural forms and vibrant colours fills the flower beds of this garden. Though many of the plants are labelled it is almost impossible to keep up with such luxuriant growth.

up a wonderful vista to the sea from a staircase that leads down from the modern part of the hotel.

Recent plantings made by Hannelore Ferreira of prodigious quantities of bromeliads have given back the garden something of its old botanical wonder. Long-suffering houseplants retired from duty in the quiet corridors are given a new lease of life in massive drifts. One particular stalwart, a stiff and prickly urn plant, *Aechmea fasciata*, is used under root-hungry palms for a full 100-metre walk. It gains tremendous elegance as hundreds of pink pineapple flowers rise above the silver foliage. Deeply shaded areas under old mango trees have been transformed from dismal corners that embarrassed the gardeners by vibrant red clumps of *Guzmania sanguinea* and *Vriesea splendens* accompanied by anthuriums.

Often eschewed for their ferocious thorns, this garden presents succulent plants in a soft and gentle guise. Above the cliffs of the west side there is a walk of silver and grey plants that incorporates many interesting shapes and forms. Form takes precedence over colour in a monochrome exercise that resembles black and white art photography. *Yucca rostrata* is one of the most striking shapes with ribbon-like leaves of an aluminium brightness. Massive rosettes of soft *Agave attenuata* produce swans' necks of white flowers that overhang the stairways from the rocks above. Ground cover is provided by 'chalksticks', a senecio (*Kleinia* or *Senecio serpens*) with blue-grey leaves shaped like clustered fingers. The islanders value this plant as an eye salve or balsam.

Further along the path is a large group of aloes in which the gardeners' instinct for collectionism overtakes all pretension to design; each individual plant jostles for attention in a way to make purist aesthetes shudder. But such is the appeal to those that appreciate plants that this is one of the most visited of all garden beds.

BELOW Pink pelargoniums
and grey-leaved helichrysum
harmonise with the buildings
newly-painted livery.

RIGHT The original rocky
character of the headland
can nowadays only be
appreciated from sea level.
The garden thrives in an
artificial paradise.

It is in fact something to contend with in garden design, certain plants demand attention and their use can slow progress along a path, punctuating a walk with infinite detail. Along with the aloes are also groups of many kinds of kalanchoes, crassulas and other tiny treasures.

The noisy passage of an escaped parrot flapping through the palm trees will sometimes divert attention away from such minutiae. Up amongst the trees are many astonishing sights. Jacarandas and the flame of the forest (*Spathodea campanulata*) vie in brilliance. The tall silky oaks (*Grevillea robusta*) are covered with burnt orange inflorescences which would make fabulous cut flowers – if only they could be reached. They are dripping with nectar that attracts many birds with no such problem of access. A curious tree, *Kigelia pinnata*, bears long salami-shaped fruits hanging just as in a smokehouse. Its dark blood-red flowers fall to the ground all around it. In the wild this attracts antelopes to feed on them, and leopards wait in the branches. The flowers are pollinated by bats. Quite a menagerie.

The palm collection has grown from the original nucleus of date palms still growing on the highest point of the headland. Seen with unexpected familiarity at eye level from the cocktail bar the great plumes of the elegant palm (*Archontophoenix cunninghamiana*) and the bright green fans of *Livistona chinensis* give the impression of taking a gin and tonic in some Malay treehouse. Back at ground level thickets of the bamboo-like parlour palm (*Chamaedorea*) crowd the small paths that criss-cross the garden beds and a number of recently-planted species show youthful promise. Along with the palms there are other similar-looking exotics: cycads with centenarian trunks, and colourful topknots of dracaenas and cordylines that flourish from a host of canes.

The garden has a healthy population of Madeira's own *Dracaena draco* or dragon tree. While none are of particular age or dimension, this is one of the few gardens in which large dragon trees may be appreciated in groups. There is a line of quite respectable specimens by the path from the hotel to the Villa Cliff (now a restaurant). They are growing in an empty flower bed covered in tuff (volcanic ash) that enables a clear appreciation of their extraordinary architecture. Behind them, protecting the over-curious from falling off the cliff, is a tremendous hedge combining great clumps of *Aloe arborescens* and terrific tangles of purple bougainvillea. The aloes are called 'Christmas rockets' by the gardeners for their fiery-red candelabras at that time of the year. The combination of red and purple with clear blue winter skies is an unforgettable sight for New Year's revellers.

BELOW Pink pelargoniums and grey-leaved helichrysum harmonise with the buildings newly-painted livery.

26. Ribeiro Frio

ABOVE The giant Madeira sow thistle, *Sonchus fruticosus*.

TOP RIGHT The forester's cottage has a small garden of box hedges planted with tree ferns.

BOTTOM RIGHT Madeira's shrubby yellow foxglove, *Isoplexis sceptrum*.

Before settlement of the island there were no freshwater fish on Madeira. How could they get there? Not by swimming across the sea. Only the eel, ambivalent in its habits and indifferent to salt water, had gained a toehold in the seasonal torrents that pass for rivers. But whether for sport or for food trout were introduced to the clear mountain streams and now lurk warily in mill ponds and the slowly flowing *levadas*.

Thanks to this tasty trespasser many of the island's rarest plants gained sanctuary at a time when little thought was given to their conservation. New roads opening up the north side of the island in the 1950s were threatening pristine forest habitats and the unique plants that they contained. Eduardo de Campos Andrade, for many years head of the Regional Forestry Service, had the idea of planting a garden reserve of Madeira wild flowers around the trout hatcheries at Ribeiro Frio, on the northern slopes of the island. This was established in 1960.

Mildred Blandy, writing in the *Journal of the Royal Horticultural Society* in 1965, praised these efforts. The shrubby yellow foxglove of Madeira (*Isoplexis sceptrum*) was probably saved from oblivion by this little garden; twenty plants raised there have become the grandparents of countless examples planted along *levada* walks by the forest services. Truly wild plants are precious few. Like so many of the *laurisilva*'s treasures, it is most exacting in its growing requirements. The sheltered humid conditions of the Ribeiro Frio ravine are difficult to reproduce elsewhere and native habitats of open woodland have all but disappeared.

In this garden, along with the isoplexis can be found Madeira spotted orchids (*Dactylorhiza foliosa*), woodwardia ferns, shrubby Madeira daisies (*Argyranthemum pinnatifidum*) and characteristic giant herbs such as *Euphorbia mellifera* and *Sonchus fruticosus*. A good labelled selection of the woody plants of the forest can also be encountered at close hand. This is just as well, since only with long acquaintance can they be distinguished one from another.

Just by the sparkling tanks of trout there is a small traditional boxwood garden from which there are neck-cricking views of the forested peaks above. The panorama is vertiginous, but watch your step. Mounds of white daisies shove through the hedges, and bunches of *Geranium palmatum* will trip your feet. Tree ferns are interlopers but add to the wondrous scene.

A visit to this garden is best begun from top to bottom. Someone will have to drop you off and wait below to pick you up, but there is a pleasant log cabin bar with a fire in the winter and trout for lunch. From Funchal and Monte, once over the mountains, the steeply descending forest road passes through managed ranks of foreign conifers before it changes suddenly to a tangled woodland of glossy laurels. This is Ribeiro Frio. There are a few lay-bys at the top for picnics and sightseeing. Surrounded by gardens of agapanthus and hydrangea and sprinkled with bright orange and yellow montbretia, these are still a long walk from the garden proper. Better to wait for the sight of wild orchids along the roadside that announce the reserve.

The trout hatchery is the starting point for a number of carefully mapped mountain walks accompanying watercourses and ravines to further wilderness. Follow the forest paths paved with shards of basalt and lined by crinkle-crankle fences to discover the spectacular landscape of the north coast.

27. Santa Catarina Park

In 1835 a law was passed prohibiting burial in the churchyards. Anti-clerical feeling in Portugal mixed with new hygienic consciousness promoted the foundation of public cemeteries. Funchal selected a hillside on the (then) outskirts of town, alongside a chapel dedicated by the city's founder, Zarco, to Saint Catherine. The cemetery was maintained for just over a hundred years.

Funchal was founded in the fifteenth century. Densely laid out, the city is almost medieval, with little public open space. Up until the late nineteenth century two small public walks sufficed the gentry for their evening promenades. The demolition of the Franciscan monastery provided the city with a fashionable public square in the 1880s (Funchal Public Garden, see p. 56) but by the mid-twentieth century a more drastic solution was adopted. The town converted the spectacularly located cemetery to a public park.

LEFT The wide spreading lawn that replaced the public cemetery is one of the largest open spaces in the city of Funchal. Tall araucarias against the skyline are growing in the garden of the Quinta Vigia.

BELOW A traditional mixture of cottage garden flowers and subtropical bedding fills the tightly packed and intensely colourful flower beds of the park.

BELOW A large artificial lake occupies the upper part of the park. It is surrounded by palms and pepper trees (a handsome subtropical substitute for the weeping willow).

TOP RIGHT The African tulip tree, *Spathodea campanulata*, was introduced to Madeira from tropical Africa.

BOTTOM RIGHT The Chapel of Santa Catarina was founded in 1425 by Constança Rodriguez, wife of the island's discoverer, Zarco. It lies at the south-eastern corner of the park, overlooking the harbour.

Fashionable Funchal had developed westwards and enveloped the new cemetery. In 1939 the bones and monuments were dug up and translated to Saint Martin's (now ironically also surrounded by new development). The city worked hard to build its new park from 1946 until finally completed in 1966. According to a statement made by its designer, Miguel Jacobetty Rosa (1901–70) the park was based on the botanic garden in Edinburgh. Both have wonderful views, but this seems a rather far-fetched comparison.

Today the gardens are a spacious, colourful tribute to traditional Madeira gardening. Giant cycads bedded with gaudy cannas and rowdy China asters will raise the eyebrows of most genteel gardeners. These plantings owe nothing to Gertrude Jekyll or

Penelope Hobhouse. Indeed they are certainly pre-Robinsonian with their jam-tart patterns, trimmed with iresine and dotted with clamorous yuccas. Interestingly new plantings along the roadside, made by the city landscape architects, have given a contemporary dimension to this concept. The huge ribbon beds of chlorophytum and *Tradescantia pallida*, agapanthus and *Pentas lanceolata* or other pairs of striking contrast, have been drawn with a largesse that surpasses the genre, creating a decidedly modern feel to the design.

Overlooking the port there are steeply terraced walks and rocky scarps that contain masses of interesting plants growing in a less disciplined manner. Perhaps it is here that Edinburgh shows its influence? Botanic variety is found in alphabetical abundance: acalypha, aloes and agaves hang off the cliffs amongst torrents of bougainvillea that pour down to the ocean, beaucarneas, begonias and bauhinias, cannas, callistemon, cycas and cereus cactus lead on to dasylirion, doryanthes and *Dracaena draco* (dragon tree); just to mention the first four letters of the alphabet.

Calmer scenes are to be enjoyed on the flat land at the cliff top. An artificial lake patrolled by swans provides the foreground to a vista of the forested mountains that surround Funchal. Snow-topped peaks shine in the clear skies of January and February. They are rarely visible throughout the rest of the year as they are wrapped by the rain clouds that provide water for the abundant gardens of lower altitudes. An enormous lawn occupies the centre of the park providing a venue for pop concerts and popular *festas*.

28. Santa Clara

Ring at the gate and you will be welcomed into one of Madeira's most hallowed spaces.

Founded by Zarco's son around the chapel where his father was buried, the convent was built between 1489 and 1496. It has functioned almost continuously from that time. Today it houses a community of nuns who run an extremely lively school and orphanage. Most visitors are content to gaze at the wonderful church interior completely covered with yellow and blue *azulejo* tiles, but there are many treasures within the rambling buildings that surround the central cloister.

This cloister may lay claim to be the oldest garden on the island. It is just as might be imagined of a 500-year-old monastic garth and certainly has never been 'restored' nor designed. The square of earth occupied by odd little flower beds lacks the typical four-quartered structure canonical to garden historians, but it is loaded with symbolism in its flowers and tended with devotion.

Roses, the flower of Mary, fill this garden. Not revered ancient cultivars, nor graded to colour and stature, but simply popular showy varieties; the people of Madeira love roses above all other flowers and cannot comprehend a garden without them. In other gardens strelitzias and heliconias are grown for profit, but here

RIGHT An arcaded walk
shelters a multitude of
cherished garden plants:
begonias, crotons, aloes,
palms and cycads.

roses are grown for sheer joy. Madonna lilies too are to be
found in season, followed later by *Lilium longiflorum*, as pure
a Christian symbol as can be, and somewhat better suited to
the local climate. Passionflowers climb the walls and arches.
Found in all Funchal gardens, here they are seen from their
original perspective: as emblems of Christ's Passion.

A second enclosure serves as the kitchen garden. This
is in a part of the convent not usually shown to visitors. It
is a pleasant jumble of cabbages and bananas, with green
beans climbing poles and everywhere the wandering vines
of a peculiar edible gourd called *pimpinella*. The earth is
formed into channels and basins so that the vegetables may
be watered by a fast-flowing stream, in a technique that has
survived all over Portugal since Moorish times.

The Franciscan sisters were the first of Madeira's tourist
entrepreneurs. Nearly all nineteenth-century accounts and
travel journals relate of visits to the convent. Artificial flowers
manufactured from the feathers of a seabird called by locals
freira (appropriately meaning the nun) were sold as souvenirs
and by all accounts were highly realistic. Unfortunately none
of this ephemeral flora has survived for us to judge today.

But the biggest attraction of the convent was Maria
Clementina, known as the 'Beautiful Nun'. Her story had
been first told in 1826 by Henry Nelson Coleridge, nephew
and son-in-law of the poet. After beseeching his readers to
buy 'the prettiest flowers for your sweetheart's hair', he
tells how Maria Clementina, a beautiful young girl hated
by her ugly sisters, had been cloistered up at an early age.
The poor unfortunate was released during a period of liberal
government and had been about to marry when politics
changed and she was locked up again. Coleridge had been so
infatuated with her that he contemplated kidnap. The story
was retold, more and more incredibly, and embroidered as
her beauty faded, until in 1867, at the end of her long life and
still a nun, she passed into legend.

29. Vila Porto Mare

Not so long ago all the land to the west of Funchal was covered with endless terraces of bananas. From sea level up to about 200 metres in altitude they covered every available patch of earth, the quaint pyramid-shaped roofs of the farmers' cottages scarcely visible above their broad green leaves. With the rapid expansion of the city in the last decades of the twentieth century, this exotic scene was replaced by blocks of high-rise apartments and new roads. Not as bad as it sounds – this is after all still Madeira – the wide avenues are lined with splendid flowering trees and there are many new parks and public gardens. But the bananas have gone. And with them a landscape that was characteristic of the city.

The last of the bananas stand in front of the Hotel Vila Porto Mare: 400 of the most photographed plants on the island. No tourist can resist a portrait standing under their leafy canopy with a huge bunch of yellow fruit draped over one shoulder. The fruit finds its way to their breakfast table and the hotel manager jokes that he will be the last member of the Banana Growers Cooperative.

The bananas were not part of the original garden design. My brief had been to keep spaces open, and planting low, so as not to obscure sea views. But as the garden progressed the brief evolved. Antonio Trindade, the hotel group's administrator, became more and more enthusiastic about the contribution that plants could make to the resort's atmosphere. Large areas that had been designated as lawn were

LEFT Tropical plants flower throughout the year in this warm sheltered garden. Cannas and *Bougainvillea* 'Mini Thai' are here backed by sabal palms.

BELOW The lawns of this garden contain the largest collection of palm species on the island.

BELOW, RIGHT AND FAR RIGHT The exotic foliage that fills these gardens is carefully blended to achieve a controlled effect of tropical luxuriance without overwhelming the limited space available.

converted to flower beds. As a result, the three shipping containers of plants sent over from the mainland, Spain, Southern France and Italy were emptied before the garden was half-finished. Local nurseries on Madeira were scoured and also soon exhausted of supplies. Then, three days before the New Year's Eve opening, the entrance area in front of the hotel was completed, ready for planting. There were no plants left.

The solution that I proposed was not an easy one to accept: let's buy a field of bananas. To the inhabitants of Madeira, the banana is anything but exotic. Banana groves are not regarded as things of beauty. To place one in front of a smart new hotel is equivalent to planting a field of potatoes in front of the Ritz. But Trindade knows his clients. He jumped at the suggestion without a moment's hesitation. Today it is common to see bananas planted in all the island's hotels.

The rest of the gardens are set out on three or four different levels. These are largely made up of roof gardens built over hotel rooms below. It is remarkable the growth that has been achieved in such a short space of time. In particular the large collection of palm species has made spectacular progress, some specimens reaching a trunk height of six metres in less than five years.

Recently the gardens have been 'adopted' by well-known Madeira ecologist Raimundo Quintal. He has classified the plant collection, labelled the specimens and even maintains a blog concerning the garden. This is a measure of the interest shown by the hotel guests who had been constantly looking for more information about the plants. Quintal has introduced new features to the garden reflecting topical concern over our planet's future and bringing a more local flavour to the resort. In particular some of the exotic flower beds have been converted, not quite to potato fields, but to vegetable gardens containing typical island crops.

Gardens to visit

Nearly all the gardens are in and around the city of Funchal, easily reached by public transport or a short taxi ride. Cable cars from the old town will take you to Monte, a hill town above the city. A further ride takes you on to the Botanic Gardens or you can return to town from Monte by basket-sled and then walk. Private gardens are opened strictly by appointment only. Hotel gardens are generally open only to their guests, though many run guided tours for visitors. It is advisable to check the information given here as it is liable to change.

Blandy Gardens
Quinta do Palheiro Ferreiro
Caminho Quinta do Palheiro 32
Sáo Gonçalo 9050-255 Funchal
On road to Camacha, 15 minutes drive
    from Funchal
Tel 291 793044
Buses 36A & 37
Admission €10, children €4
09h00 – 16h30, Monday to Friday,
    closed Christmas
www.palheiroestate.com/lang-en/
    gardens/welcome.html

Botanic Gardens
Jardim Botanico de Funchal
Quinta do Bom Sucesso
Caminho do Meio, 9050 – 244 Funchal
Buses 29, 30, 31, 31A
Cable car from Monte
Admission €3
09h00 – 18h00 every day except
    Christmas
www.sra.pt/jarbot/

Burial Ground and English Church
Cemitério dos Ingleses
Rua da Carreira 235 (ring at small green
    gate)
8h00 – 17h00, closed Saturday, Sunday
    & holidays
Holy Trinity Church
Rua Quebra Costas 20, 9000-034
    Funchal
www.holytrinity-madeira.org

Dragon Tree Sanctuary
Núcleo de Dragoeiros das Neves

Estrada Regional 204
Tel 291 795155
Centro de Informação do Serviço
    do Parque Natural da Madeira
Caminho da Portadas, São Gonçalo
9050-297 Funchal
Tel 291 793803

Ecological Park
Parque Ecológico do Funchal
Centro de Recepção
Estrada Regional 103, no. 259
Ribeira das Cales, 9050 Funchal
pecof@cm-funchal.pt
Associação dos Amigos do Parque
    Ecológico do Funchal
Jardins do Monte, 9050-208 Funchal,
    Madeira
Buses 103, 56
amigosdoparque@gmail.com

Funchal Public Garden
Jardim Municipal do Funchal
Avenida Arriaga, 9000-060 Funchal
Open 24 hours, 7 days a week

Hospice of the Princess Amelia
Companhia das Filhas da Caridade de S.
    Vicente de Paulo
Avenida do Infante 12, 9000-015
    Funchal
Tel 291 236382, Fax 291 229 449
08h00 – 20h00
hospprincesaamelia@netmadeira.com

Madeira Magic
Rua Ponta da Cruz, 25
9000-103 Funchal
Tel 291 700 708
Buses 1, 2, 4, 24, 35, 48
Admission €4, family €12
10h00 – 18h00, closed Mondays, 24, 25,
    31 December, 1 January
www.madeira-magic.com

Monte Palace
The Berardo Foundation
Jardim Tropical Monte Palace
Caminho Monte 174, 9050-288 Funchal
Tel 291 742 650
Buses 20, 21 22, 48
Cable car from Old Town, Funchal
Admission €10, children under 15 free
09h30 – 18h00 every day, closed
    Christmas

www.montepalace.com
www.berardocollection.com

Monte Public Garden
Parque Leite Monteiro
Largo da Fonte, Monte,
    9050-208 Funchal
Cable car from Old Town
Buses 20, 21, 48
Open 24 hours, 7 days a week

Quinta do Arco
Sítio da Lagoa
9230-018 Arco de S. Jorge
Tel 291 570 250
Bus 103 Funchal – Arco de São Jorge
Admission €5
10h00 – 18h00, open from April to
    December
info@quintadoarco.com
www.quintadoarco.com

Quinta da Boa Vista
Rua Lombo da Boa Vista
9050-126 Funchal
Tel 291 220 468, Fax 291 230 309
Bus 32 or short walk from city centre
Admission €3.50 – 1 February to 31
    May, €2.50 – 1 June to 31 January
09h00 – 17h30, Monday to Saturday,
    closed Sundays and public holidays
www.madeira-tourist.com/page0/
    page8/page8.html

Quinta das Cruzes
Museu Quinta das Cruzes
Calçada do Pico 9000 – 206 Funchal
Tel 291 740 670, Fax 291 741 384
09h00 – 17h00, Monday to Friday
mqc.drac@madeira-edu.pt
www.museuquintadascruzes.com/en-
    GB/Default.aspx

Quinta Magnolia
Rua Dr. Pita, 9000-089 Funchal
08h00 – 20h00, every day except
    Christmas and New Year

Quinta do Monte
Caminho do Pico, Monte, 9050-482
    Funchal
Tel 291 780 460, Fax 291 780 465
Admission €6
09h30 – 17h30, Monday to Saturday,
    closed Sundays

Quinta da Palmeira
Rua da Levada de Santa Luzia 31 A
9050-430 Funchal
Tel 291 221 091
Admission €5
09h00 – 12h00 and 14h00 – 17h00,
    Monday to Friday

Quinta Vigia
Residência Oficial do Senhor Presidente
    do Governo Regional.
Avenida do Infante 1, 9004-547 Funchal
09h00 – 17h00, Monday to Friday

Ribeiro Frio
Parque Florestal do Ribeiro Frio
Estrada Regional 103
(15 km from Funchal)
Ribeiro Frio
9230-209 São Roque do Faial
Tel 291 575434
Buses 103, 56

Santa Catarina Park
Av. do Infante, 9000-015 Funchal
07h00 – 21h00, 22 March to 22
    September, 08h00 – 19h00, 23
    September to 21 March
ParquesJardinsCemiterios@cm-
    funchal.pt

Santa Clara
Calçada de Santa Clara 15, 9000-036
    Funchal
Tel 291 742 602
Admission €2
10h00 – 12h00 and 15h00 – 17h00

Hotels
Blandy Gardens – www.casa-velha.com
Choupana Hills –
    www.choupanahills.com
Jardins do Lago –
    www.jardinsdolago.com
Miramar – www.pestana.com
Pestana Grand – www.pestana.com
Pestana Village – www.pestana.com
Quinta do Arco –
    www.quintadoarco.com
Reid's – www.reidspalace.com
Vila Portomar – www.portobay.com

Bibliography

Thanks are due to librarians and archivists at the following libraries for assistance with my research: Arquivo Regional da Madeira; Biblioteca de Culturas Estrangeiras (Quinta Magnolia); Biblioteca Municipal de Funchal (Hinton Collection); Biblioteca Nacional, Lisbon; Casa Museu Frederico Freitas, Funchal; Lindley Library, London.

Introduction

ANON, *An historical account of the discovery of the island of Madeira, abridged from the Portugueze original. To which is added, an account of the present state of the island, in a letter to a friend*, London: printed for J. Payne & J. Bouquet, 1748.
BARROS, João de, *Asia*, Lisbon: Regia Officina Typografica, 1578.
COSTA, A. and FRANQUINHO, L., *Madeira: plantas e flores*, Funchal: Francisco Ribeiro & Filhos, 1986.
OVINGTON, John, *A voyage to Suratt in the year 1689: giving a large account of that city and its inhabitants and of the English factory there: likewise a description of Madiera …,* London: Jacob Tonson, 1696.
PENFOLD, Jane Wallas, *Madeira flowers, fruits, and ferns, a selection of the botanical productions of that island, foreign and indigenous, drawn and coloured from nature*, London: Reeve Bros., 1845.
SILVA, Fernando Augusto da, and MENESES, Carlos Azevedo de, *Elucidário Madeirense*, Funchal: Tip. Esperança, 1940–1946.
SHORE, Emily, *Journal of Emily Shore*, London: Kegan Paul, Trench Trübner & Co., 1891.
SLOANE, Sir Hans, *A voyage to the islands Madera, Barbados, Nieves, S. Christophers and Jamaica …*, London: printed by B.M. for the author, 1707–1725.
SZIEMER, Peter, *Eine kurze Naturgeschichte Madeiras / Madeira Natural History in a Nutshell,* Funchal: Francisco Ribeiro & Filhos, 2000.

Blandy Gardens

BLANDY, Mildred, 'Quinta do Palheiro: a Madeira garden', in *Journal of the Royal Horticultural Society*, 1955, p.400.
BURTS, Robert, *Around the world: a narrative of a voyage in the East India Squadron under Commodore George C. Read*, vol. I, New York: Charles S. Francis, 1840, p.90
DRIVER, John, *Letters from Madeira in 1834: with an appendix illustrative of the*
island, climate, wines and other information up to the year 1838, London: Longman & Co., 1838.
STANFORD, Sir Charles Thomas, Bt., *Leaves from a Madeira garden*, London: John Lane, The Bodley Head, 1909.
THOMSON, James, *The Castle of Indolence*, Canto I, London: A. Millar, 1748.

Botanic Gardens

NEVES, Henrique Costa, *Laurisilva da Madeira,* Funchal: Parque Natural da Madeira, 1996.
JARDIM, Roberto and FRANCISCO, David, *Flora Endémica da Madeira, Endemic Flora of Madeira*, Funchal: Múchia, 2000.
PRESS, J.R. and SHORT, M., *Flora of Madeira*, London: Natural History Museum, 1994.

Burial Ground and English Church

LOWE, Richard Thomas, *A Manual Flora of Madeira and the adjacent Islands of Porto Santo and the Dezertas*, London, 1857.

Dragon Tree Sanctuary

FRUTUOSO, Gaspar, *Saudades da Terra*, Ponta Delgada: Instituto Cultural de Ponta Delgada, 2005.
MASON, Peter, 'A dragon tree in the Garden of Eden' in *Journal of the History of Collections*, Vol. 18(2), 2006, pp.169–85.
PAZ-SÁNCHEZ, M. de, 'Un drago en El Jardín de las Delicias', in M. de Paz-Sánchez (ed.), *Flandes y Canarias. Nuestros orígenes nórdicos*, vol. I, 2004.

Funchal Public Garden

SITWELL, Sacheverell, *Portugal and Madeira*, London: B.T. Batsford, 1954.
[illustration] 'View in the Public Gardens, Madeira', in *Gardeners' Chronicle*, series 3 vol. 4, 1888, facing p.386.
GRABHAM, Michael, *Plants seen in Madeira: a handbook of botanical information for visitors and intending residents*, London: H.K. Lewis, 1934.

Jardins do Lago

ROBLEY, Augusta J., *A selection of Madeira flowers, drawn and coloured from nature, and dedicated to her mother, Mrs. Penfold, of the Açhada, Madeira*, London: Reeve Brothers, 1845.
WORDSWORTH, William, 'Fair lady! can I sing of flowers', 1845 in *The*
Complete Poetical works, Vol. IX *Last Poems*, Boston: Houghton Mifflin, 1919.

Madeira Magic

LUCKHURST, Gerald, *Magic Garden Guide – Exploring the Flora of Madeira*, Funchal, 2006

Miramar

ROPER, Frances A., *Visit to Madeira 25th Sept – 9th Oct 1954,* http://www.anotherurl.com/photos/family/old_hubbard/madeira/journal.asp

Monte Palace

CARVALHO, Marta, *Monte Palace A Tropical Garden*, Funchal: José Berardo Foundation, 1999.

Pestana Village

QUINTAL, Raimundo, *Quintas, Parques e Jardins do Funchal: estudo fitogeográfico*, Lisbon: Esfera do Caos, 2007.

Quinta do Arco

ALBUQUERQUE, Miguel, *Roseiras Antigas de Jardim*, Lisbon: Alêtheia, 2006.

Quinta Magnolia

FRANÇA, Isabella de, *Journal of a visit to Madeira and Portugal (1853–1854)*, Funchal: Junta Geral do Distrito Autónomo, 1970.
MARCH, Charles Wainwright, *Sketches and adventures in Madeira, Portugal, and the Andalusias of Spain*, New York: Harper & Brothers, 1856.
McLANATHAN, Richard B.K., 'The Collection of Ship Models', *Bulletin of the Museum of Fine Arts*, Vol. 54, No. 298 (Winter, 1956), pp.93–99 [*Figurehead of ship 'Creole'*, Museum of Fine Arts, Boston, Accession number: 32.172].
WATNEY, Herbert, Album of photographs, 1898, archives of The Mercers' Company, Mercers Hall, Ironmonger Lane, London EC2V 8HE.

Quinta da Palmeira

HARCOURT, Edward Vernon, *A sketch of Madeira: containing information for the traveller, or invalid visitor*, London: Murray, 1851.
HOARE, Majorie, *The quintas of Madeira*, Funchal: Francisco Ribeiro & Filhos, 2004.
MILES, Cecil, *A glimpse of Madeira*, London: P. Garnett, 1949.
TAYLOR, George Crosbie, *Garden*
making by example, London: Country Life, 1932.

Reid's

WEAVER, H.J. *Reid's Hotel: Jewel of the Atlantic*, London: Souvenir Press, 1991

Ribeiro Frio

BLANDY, Mildred, 'Isoplexis sceptrum, The Yellow Foxglove of Madeira' in *Journal of the Royal Horticultural Society*, vol. 177, 1965, pp.400–401.

Santa Clara

COLERIDGE, Henry Nelson, *Six months in the West Indies in 1825*, London: J. Murray, 1826.

Vila Porto Mare

QUINTAL, Raimundo and Pais, António, *The Garden of Vila Porto Mare* http://vpmgardens.blogspot.com.

Picture Credits

All photographs are by the author unless indicated below

p.18 above
Biblioteca Nacional Digital, Lisbon, Portugal

p.18 below
RHS Lindley Library, London

pp.110–111
Biblioteca de Culturas Estrangeiras, Quinta Magnólia, Funchal

p.119 below
Casa Museu Frederico de Freitas, Funchal

Photographs by Henrique Seruca
© Henrique Seruca / Madeira Tourism
pp.12–13, 34–35, 62, 63 (both images), 114, 127 (both images), 157

Index